THE STATISTICAL PROFILE ON NEPALESE WOMEN

An Update
in the Policy Context

Institute for Integrated Development Studies
P. O. Box: 2254
Baneswor, Kathmandu

August, 1994

Published by: Institute For Integrated Development Studies
                 P. O. Box 2254
                 Baneswor, Kathmandu, Nepal.
                 Tel.: 474718
                 Fax: 977-1-470831

Copyright: 1994, Institute for Integrated Development Studies

Designed by: WordScape Naxal, Kathmandu Tel. 410290

Printed by: Modern Printing Press, Tel. 214886

TABLE OF CONTENTS

List of Tables

ACKNOWLEDGEMENTS

Work on this book commenced when the preliminary report of the census 1991 started to come out. Several of my colleagues worked intensively on this project during the last two years. Ms. Sangeeta Khatri and Mr. Badri Niraula helped me to write the original draft. Together with Mr. Ashwasthama Pokhrel, these two colleagues were responsible for condensing the tables from the original census data. Ms. Anju Chetri and the Asmita group helped me in the cover design. UNICEF was generous enough to let me use their file photos. My sincere thanks to all of them; without their contributions this book would not have taken the shape it did. The Central Bureau of Statistics allowed use of computer printouts even before the publication of the census report. The Bureau and its Director, Mr. K. R. Sharma, therefore, deserve due acknowledgement.

I owe a special measure of gratitude to the Canadian Cooperation Office for extending its financial contribution beyond the project to the publication stage.

Finally, all my colleagues in the IIDS computer pool, particularly Mr. Binod Adhikari, deserve special appreciation for bearing with the demands that the manuscript made in typing and retyping; their patience has paid off.

I. INTRODUCTION

1.1 Background

When women became a major thrust in development in the mid-seventies, data on women's lives and life options in Nepal was scarce. Till then, women's issues were viewed purely from a welfare perspective. *The Status of Women* in Nepal study series, published between 1979-1981, attempted an analysis of the role of women in various walks of life. Their economic contributions, life options and general status were reviewed in a multi-dimensional framework. This series was published in two segments. The first portion, consisting of five volumes, analyzed various aspects of women's status from existing sources. In this in-depth studies process, gaps in information were identified. During the second stage, detailed case studies were carried out in eight villages with a view to gather additional data and probe deeper into various dimensions of the status issue. In doing so, both quantitative as well as qualitative methods were adopted. The study was successful in establishing that women constituted the backbone of Nepalese agriculture, specially in the hill areas. Their contribution to household production and income was found to be at par with men, both in terms of labor input as well as in decision making roles. (See Fig. 1.1 & 1.2)

The social status of women and their access to resources varied widely depending on the cultural group they belonged to. Generally, women belonging to Tibeto-Burman cultural groups had considerably greater freedom in matters such as choice of marriage partners, deciding the time for marriage and in selection of economic activities they wished to pursue, as compared to their sisters belonging to the Indo-Aryan cultural group. The Tibeto-Burman groups included in the study were Mustang Bhote (Tibetan) women, Kham Magars, Rais and Tamangs. The Indo-Aryan group included high and low caste Nepali-speaking hill groups, as well as Maithili, Tharus and Newars. While Indo-Aryan women were married early, had no choice in their life partners and were severely restricted in their social mobility, such findings did not generally apply to women belonging to Tibetan-Burman groups. In all cultural groups, however, it was found that women's access to modern resources in the form of knowledge (education, training, etc.,) and traditional and newly created assets (e.g.land, machines, employment) was severely limited.

Fig 1.1 Male/Female Contribution to Household Income

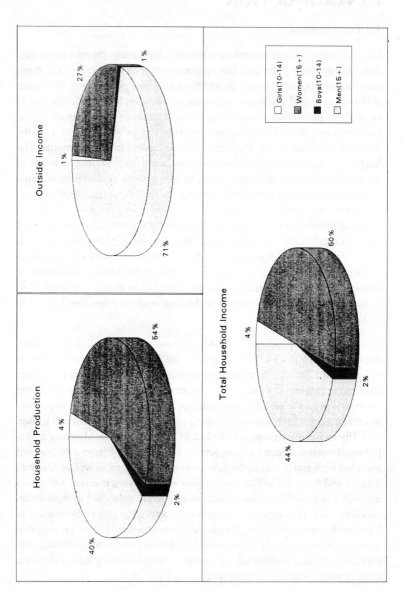

Source: Acharya & Bennett, 1981

Fig 1.2 Decision Making Roles

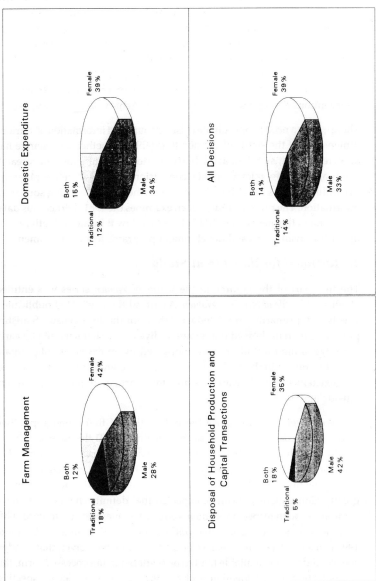

Farm Management

Domestic Expenditure

Disposal of Household Production and Capital Transactions

All Decisions

Source: Acharya & Bennett, 1981

Neither the substantial contributions of women in labor input and management of household production nor their progressive marginalization from modern forms of asset ownership and employment avenues was reflected in the available secondary statistics. Accordingly, a major recommendation running through the *Status of Women* study series called for improving statistical methods of data gathering and processing so as to underline the differential in impact of various developmental interventions among men and women. (See Acharya and Bennett, 1981.)

There is now a need to re-evaluate existing sources of information on various dimensions of the status of women to establish whether any change has occurred in terms of data availability, to identify data gaps and research needs and to draw relevant policy conclusions. IIDS is therefore planning to conduct a series of studies on women on the basis of existing sources of information. The present study, which examines the 1981, 1991 census data, is the first in this new series. IIDS plans to follow it by an in-depth review of various institutions and development programs related to women.

1.2 Rational for the Current Study

The first part of the volume in the *Status of Women* series was entitled *"Statistical Profile of Nepalese Women: A Critical Review"*. That publication was based, primarily, on secondary data from the 1971 census. Statistics presented therein showed that women's lives were characterized by early marriage, a high fertility rate accompanied by an extremely high infant mortality rate, a high death rate, low life expectancy, a low literacy rate, non-existent political awareness and low participation in employment outside agriculture.

It is well over a decade since the publication of that monograph. Two censuses have been conducted since then, one in 1981 the other in 1991. In the 20 years that have elapsed since 1971 a new generation of women has come of age. Additional areas of the country have been opened up by new roads. The number of schools and public health facilities have expanded greatly. Consequently, it can be expected that definite changes may have come about with respect to women's education, marriage patterns and life options. The need to update that publication, incorporating the 1981 and 1991 censuses, has hence been strongly felt. Moreover, given that gender-specific data when available tend to be scattered in unprocessed form, this needs to be brought together and analyzed from a gender perspective.

4

Other women-related studies, too, can refer to such basic data as can be provided by this updating of the earlier statistical profile of Nepalese women. The updating process began when the preliminary results from the 1991 census were made public.

In the late seventies, specific attempts were made to involve the people in the development process. In many districts of the kingdom, programs were launched that were directed at women, in general, and at fertility control, in particular. With a multitude of public policies having been directed at the upliftment of the rural population, considerable changes may be expected in marriage patterns, fertility rates, and literacy and employment trends among women. An attempt has therefore been made to evaluate the impact of various programs on the life options of women, on the basis of available district-level data. What follows, therefore, is not merely an update of statistics and analysis of emergent patterns but an endeavour to draw a number of relevant policy conclusions on women's issues.

1.3. Objectives

Accordingly, the specific objectives of this study were:

(a) Updating The Statistical Profile of Nepalese Women with a view to providing the latest comprehensive data on women including general demographic features, social and economic characteristics and political expression in light of the 1981 and 1991 census and other sources of statistical information.

(b) To provide a comparative study of the 1971, 1981 and 1991 censuses with analysis of differences in indicators, if any, between then and the present.

(c) To evaluate the effects of micro-level interventions on the basis of comparative district-level statistics.

(d) To draw policy conclusions from the above analysis.

1.4 Methodology

The current analysis is based primarily on the 1981 and 1991 census data. Information from a number of additional sources has also been integrated in the analysis. Main additional sources consulted were: the 1991 Nepal Fertility and Family Planning Survey, the UNIDO-funded Survey on Women Industrial Workers (1988), Survey of Women Industrial Workers in the Kathmandu Valley (1991) and election results, at the central and local levels. The study is comprised mainly of appropriate tabulations with a descriptive analysis of the same. The emphasis has been placed on a few major indicators such as sex ratio, age of marriage, literacy and educational attainments, proportion of separated/divorced women, economic activity rates and the sectoral distribution of the economically active population. The educational and marital status of the organized-sector labor force, their age distribution, and their working conditions have also been analyzed where possible. The focus has been on examining trends in terms of the indicators identified in *The Statistical Profile of Nepalese Women*. A brief review of policies and programs is also included in chapter eight.

1.5 Limitations

This study has been undertaken bearing in mind the possibility of inconsistencies and unreliability of census data on women, in general, and women's economic activity, in particular. Here it should be recalled that one of the major issues that had been raised in *The Statistical Profile of Nepalese Women* was the inadequacy of census data to reflect the actual social and work status of Nepalese women. That critical issue, raised then, is still valid. As much is reflected in the inconsistency of the census series regarding various indicators such as sex ratio and economic activity rates. It has nevertheless been felt necessary to examine census data, even if only to identify those inconsistencies.

II. GENERAL DEMOGRAPHIC FEATURES

2.1 Population Growth and Regional Distribution

In 1981, Nepal's population was estimated at slightly more than 15 million. That figure increased to 18.5 million by 1991. Over the 1981-1991 decade, Nepal's population thus grew by 2.1 percent annually. The corresponding figure for the Hill region is just in the vicinity of 1.6 percent. The Mountain region population had the lowest growth rate at one percent per annum. Population growth was the most rapid in the Tarai region at the level of 2.8 percent per annum. The comparative contribution of various factors in the uneven growth of population in the three regions has yet to be studied in depth. Nevertheless, it is quite evident that the quickest growth rate of the population in the Tarai is due to internal and external migration (See Niraula, 1994 B)

One of the consequences of rapid population growth is enhanced population density. In 1991, population density was 125.6 persons per sq.km, with heaviest pressure in the Kathmandu Valley. That figure may not be very high compared to many countries. However, what must be noted is that it has increased from 56 persons per sq.km in 1952/54 to 102 persons per sq. km in 1981 and 126 persons per sq.km in 1991. (Table 2.1). Moreover the population pressure on the cultivated land is much higher.

Table 2.1 Area and Population by Geographic Region
(Census years 1971 - 1991)

Particulars	Unit	Geographic Region			
		Mountain	Hills	Tarai	Total
Total Area 1971/81/91	Sq. Km	51,817	61,345	34,019	147,181
Cultivated Area 1985	Hectare	122,587	939,704	1,401,426	2,463,717
Population					
1971	Number	1,138,610	6,071,407	4,345,966	11,555,983
1981	"	1,302,896	7,163,115	6,556,828	15,022,839
1991	"	1,443,130	8,419,889	8,628,078	18,491,097

Source: Population Census, 1971, 1981 and 1991, CBS.

7

The population density varies from region to region. The Tarai is the most densely populated while the Mountain region is the most sparsely populated. The population density in the Mountain region has increased by just over 27 percent in the last two decades. The Tarai population density, on the other hand, has almost doubled in the same period while the Hill region witnessed an increase of 38 percent. Similarly, with respect to the various development regions, the Tarai areas of the Eastern Development Region show the heaviest pressure. The Mountain area of the Western Development Region have the lowest density (Table 2.2). Since nearly two-thirds of Nepal's land area consists of hills and mountains, the greater comparative scarcity of arable land in the Hill and Mountain regions, in relation to the Tarai, would seem to explain the exodus of people from the former to the latter.

Table 2.2 Density of Population by Geographic and Development Regions

(Person per sq. km)

Geographic Region	Census Year	On Total Land						On cultivated Land
		Eastern	Central	Western	Mid Western	Far Western	Regional	
Mountain	1971	29.2	56.4	5.9	9.7	30.1	22.0	451
	1981	32.4	65.8	3.4	11.4	36.4	25.1	517
	1991	34.4	75.0	3.4	12.2	42.0	27.9	572
Hills	1971	102.9	147.5	99.2	64.6	77.2	99.0	410
	1981	116.9	178.6	117.4	76.0	89.4	116.9	484
	1991	133.0	227.0	132.2	89.0	99.2	137.3	568
Tarai	1971	190.9	189.8	113.1	54.0	40.8	127.8	352
	1981	290.7	256.0	182.1	91.7	88.1	192.7	531
	1991	365.3	325.2	252.9	127.2	139.5	253.5	699
All Nepal	1971	**98.3**	**141.0**	**83.2**	**35.1**	**49.0**	**78.5**	390
	1981	**130.3**	**179.1**	**106.4**	**46.1**	**67.6**	**102.2**	510
	1991	**156.3**	**225.6**	**128.3**	**56.9**	**85.9**	**125.6**	620

Source: Population Census, 1971, 1981 and 1991, CBS.

2.2 Language

Nepali has been and continues to be the dominant language in the country as the mother tongue of the majority of the population although no consistent trend has been observed in the relative linguistic composition of the population. The proportion of people with Nepali as mother tongue increased both numerically and in percentage terms over the 1971-1981 decade from 52.5 in 1971 to 58.3 percent in 1981. However, that figure decreased by 8 percentage points to 50.3 percent of the total in 1991.

Numerically, in all three censuses, Maithili occupied the second position. However, the percentage has shown a slight decrease from 11.5 to 11.1 in the 1991-1981 decade and an increase to 11.8 percent in 1991. Bhojpuri language speakers occupy the third position increasing slightly from about 7 percent in 1971 to 7.5 percent in 1991. Most of the other language groupings such as Newari, Tamang, Tharu, Magar, Rai/Kirati etc., have increased their shares in the 1981-1991 decade. (Table 2.3). The decline in the share of Nepali and the increase in the proportion of other language groups during the 1981-1991 period may be explained by various factors such as self-assertion by various minority language groups during reporting, uneven effect of modernization on family size of various ethnic groups, etc..

Table 2.3 Composition of Population by Mother Tongue

(Number in '000)

Language Groups	1971		1981		1991	
	Number	Percent	Number	Percent	Number	Percent
Nepali	6061	52.5	8,767	58.3	9,303	50.3
Maithili	1327	11.5	1,668	11.1	2,192	11.8
Bhojpuri	806	7.0	1,143	7.6	1,380	7.5
Newari	455	3.9	449	3.0	690	3.7
Gurung	172	1.5	174	1.2	228	1.2
Tamang	555	4.8	522	3.5	904	4.9
Abadhi	317	2.7	234	1.5	375	2.0
Tharu	496	4.3	546	3.6	993	5.4
Magar	288	2.5	213	1.4	430	2.3
Limbu	171	1.5	129	0.9	254	1.4
Rai/Kirati	232	2.0	221	1.5	439	2.4
Bhote/Sherpa			74	0.5	122	0.7
Rajbansi			59	0.4	86	0.5
Urdu					202	1.1
Hindi					171	0.9
Others/unstatedd	675	5.8	823	5.5	722	3.9
Total	**11,555**	**100.0**	**15,022**	**100.0**	**18,491**	**100.0**

Source: Population Census, 1971, 1981 and 1991, CBS.

2.3 Age Structure And Sex Ratio

In terms of its composition, the population of Nepal is becoming younger. The proportion of young males is increasing slightly faster than that of females. The percentage of the under-fifteen population has been increasing over the years with males increasing from 40.9 to 43.5 and females from 40.0 to 41.3 in the past twenty years. On the other side of the age curve, the 1991 census reveals that 5.9 percent of the total population was about 60 and above compared to 5.7 percent females (Table 2.4). As such, age-specific sex-ratios have also been changing.

Table 2.4 Composition of Population by Broad Age Group and Sex

(Percent)

Age Group	1971			1981			1991		
	Male	Female	Total	Male	Female	Total	Male	Female	Total
0 - 14	40.9	40.0	40.4	41.9	40.7	41.3	43.5	41.3	42.4
15 - 59	53.7	54.1	53.9	52.2	53.7	52.9	50.6	53.0	51.8
60 +	5.4	5.9	5.6	5.9	5.6	5.8	5.9	5.7	5.8
Total	**100.0**	**100.0**	**100.0**	**100.0**	**100.0**	**100.0**	**100.0**	**100.0**	**100.0**

Source: *Population Census, 1971, 1981 and 1991, CBS.*

The sex-ratio, defined as the number of males per 100 females, is an important indicator of women's status because it is a cumulative product of demographic and social behavior patterns. A sex ratio over 100 denotes an excess of males over females and a ratio below 100 denotes an excess of females over males. As a natural rule, there is a preponderance of male births over female births among the human population in general. By the age of five the sex ratio is considered to be equalized since, by nature, male children are physically weaker than female children and thus a smaller proportion of male survive compared to females (United Nations, 1991, p. 11). Further, universally, a larger proportion of women survive to old age, as compared to men (Ibid). Consequently, world population composition is in favor of the female of the species. However, the South Asian countries in general have had a reverse overall sex ratios due to socio-economic discrimination against the female child and women in general (Table 2.5). According to the 1991 census, in Nepal that ratio seemed to be reversing itself. Adjusted population figures, nevertheless, still show more men than women, with a sex ratio of 101.6.

10

Table 2.5 Sex Ratios in the Total Population of SAARC Countries

SAARC Countries	Year	Sex-ratio (# Males/100 females)
Nepal	1991	99.5
Bangladesh	1991a/	105.8
Bhutan	1993	104.1
India	1991	107.6
Pakistan	1990/91b/	108.6
Sri Lanka	1990	100.7

Source : Population and Housing Censuses of various countries and Demographic Year Book 1991, published by United Nations.

a/ Bangladesh Bureau of Statistics, 1993, Women and Men in Bangladesh, Facts & Figures, 1992

b/ UNFPA: Inventory of Population Projects in Developing Counties Around the World, 1990/91

In 1981, 7.3 million persons or 48.8 percent of the total population in Nepal was female. The sex ratio for the population was 105 males per 100 females. In 1991, of the 18.5 million population 9.2 million were males and 9.3 million females (Table 2.6). Thus, while the overall sex ratios observed in 1971 and 1981 were in favor of males, the 1991 census shows a slight dominance of females in the population.

Table 2.6 Population of Nepal, Census Years (1952-1991)

Census Year	Male ('000)	Female ('000)	Total ('000)	Males per 100 females
1952/54	4,250	4,223	8,473	100.6
1961	4,807	4,802	9,609	100.1
1971	5,817	5,739	11,556	101.4
1981	7,695	7,328	15,023	105.0
1991	9,221	9,270	18,491	99.5

Source: Population Census, 1971, 1981 and 1991, CBS.

However this data needs to be examined in greater depth to see if it marks a real improvement. Inter-census changes in age-specific sex ratios are not consistent. One reason for that could be under enumeration of males in the working ages between 15 and 34 as they could have migrated to urban centers in Nepal and abroad for employment. Generally, there is only a slight possibility of under enumeration of males in this age group. However, there is a much greater probability of thé mobile population being left out, both at their native place as well as at sites of temporary residence or employment. That pattern may have been accentuated further during the 1981-1991 decade. The ratio of males per 100 females has decreased almost in all age groups compared to 1991. However, the decline in the 15+ age group seems to be more pronounced. The highest sex ratio in the 1991 census is seen in the 55-59 age group followed by the 65-69 and 10-14 age groups. The sex ratio shows a rising trend up to the 10-14 age group after which it declines and then rises beyond the 30-34 age group. Age-specific sex ratios show an excess of females in the prime fertility, or 20-34, age range from 1971 through 1991. (Table 2.6). That would seem to be clear evidence of male out-migration from native areas. Since it is precisely during this period that a high proportion of women die due to maternity complications, the preponderance of women in that age group does not, therefore, seem credible.

Table 2.7 Age Specific Sex Ratios

(Males per 100 females)

Age Group	1971	1981	1991
0 - 4	93.7	105.9	102.6
5 - 9	103.3	104.1	103.9
10 - 14	118.3	116.7	108.3
15 - 19	109.5	110.0	96.0
20 - 24	92.5	91.2	85.1
25 - 29	96.3	96.4	89.3
30 - 34	90.6	92.3	91.8
35 - 39	107.8	107.1	101.0
40 - 44	98.2	100.2	94.7
45 - 49	113.9	113.9	104.0
50 - 54	104.0	115.2	105.6
55 - 59	106.6	119.3	115.8
60 - 64	88.9	109.0	99.7
65 - 69	100.6	115.8	110.1
70 - 74	91.8	112.9	105.0
75 - 79	91.9	108.4	106.0
80 +			88.8
Total	**101.4**	**105.0**	**99.5**

Source: Population Census 1971, 1981 and 1991, CBS.

Fig 2.1 Age Specific Sex Ratio
(Males per 100 Females)

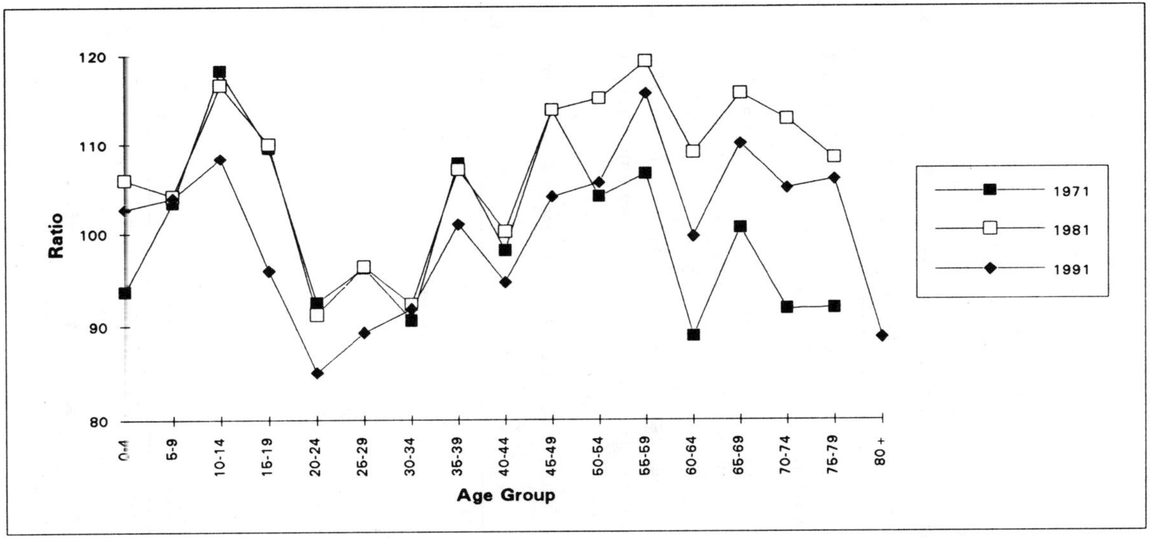

In an accurate census, out-migration from rural areas would have been reflected in regional distribution. All three geographical regions of Nepal in 1981 showed a higher male population, as compared to the female. The Tarai had the highest sex ratio both in 1981 and 1991 (Table 2.8). That could be due to several factors such as recruitment of hillmen into foreign armies and hence their under enumeration in the census. Another factor could be that most of such men migrate either to the Tarai or to the Kathmandu Valley or to India in search of better employment opportunities. The Central Hill region which includes the Kathmandu Valley definitely has more men than women. An additional reason for the highest sex ratio to obtain in the Tarai could be related to the relatively lower socio-economic status of women in Tarai communities of Indo-Aryan origin leading to a higher death rate among women. (See Acharya, 1981).

The region-wise sex ratio for the 1991 census shows a greater number of males only in the Tarai region. However, the sex ratio declined from 108.3 in 1981 to 103.9 in 1991 even in the Tarai (Table 2.7). This may indicate that the mainly-male migration to the Tarai during the seventies either petered out during the eighties or that many earlier emigrants have moved their families as well.

Table 2.8 Sex Ratio by Geographic and Development Regions

(Males per 100 females)

Geographic Region	Census Year	Eastern	Central	Western	Mid Western	Far Western	Regional
Mountain	1971	98.0	100.0	103.0	105.0	101.0	100.8
	1981	101.9	106.7	108.4	107.8	102.3	104.7
	1991	96.3	99.9	109.1	103.1	94.6	98.4
Hills	1971	97.4	100.2	95.2	97.0	98.5	98.0
	1981	101.5	106.9	99.9	100.2	98.9	102.1
	1991	96.7	101.6	88.6	96.3	91.6	95.3
Tarai	1971	107.5	105.0	106.6	107.0	110.4	106.4
	1981	108.1	107.3	108.9	107.2	115.9	108.3
	1991	103.1	106.2	102.7	102.0	101.3	103.9
All Nepal	**1971**	**102.3**	**103.3**	**97.9**	**100.8**	**100.7**	**101.4**
	1981	**105.3**	**107.1**	**102.6**	**103.5**	**104.9**	**105.0**
	1991	**100.5**	**103.7**	**93.5**	**99.2**	**96.0**	**99.5**

Source: Population Census, 1971, 1981 and 1991, CBS.

Because of the estimated under reporting of the population, the total census reported population figure has been revised upwards by the Central Bureau of Statistics for projection purposes. Actual annual growth rate of the population during the eighties has been estimated to be around 2.5 percent and total population in 1991 at 19.3 million. Of this, 9.71 million are estimated to be men and 9.56 million women, giving a sex ratio of 101.6 males per 100 females. (CBS, personal communication).

2.4 Fertility

One of the most important indicators of women's empowerment is control over their own fertility. Women's bodies have been used and abused on account of their fertility. To an extent, social control over women's sexuality is also related to their fertility. In the Hindu tradition, women are worshipped for their fertility, in the exalted status of mother-Goddess, while infertility is considered a curse (See Bennett, 1983, Kasarda, Billy and West, 1986). Pregnancies, child-birth and lactation force women to withdraw from active economic work, thus making them dependent on other members of society. Frequent pregnancies impinge on their health and sometimes even on their very lives. It is therefore most important to examine whether women have control over their own fertility. Hitherto, no research has focussed on the degree of control that women exercise over their own fertility.

Information thus far collected on the attitudes of women towards family planning and fertility control is not adequate to fully establish who controls their fertility. Social and family pressures, for example, are not reflected in such statistics. The desire for children, specially sons, who can provide women with social status and power, is internalized since their early childhood. The socially acceptable role for women is only through marriage and motherhood. As her fertility is the end product of these complex social processes, it may be considered as an indicator whether or not such processes are changing.

Statistics on fertility are conflicting and continuously reestimated by various sources. According to the nation-wide 1991 Survey on Fertility, Family Planning and Health (NFHS), there has hardly been any change in the completed marital fertility rates between 1971-76 and 1991 (See Table 2.9). That is quite surprising given the huge amount of resources that has been expended on family planning programs in the past 20 years. Although awareness about family planning methods is reported to be high (Table 2.10), their use and end effect on marital fertility seem only to be marginal. That is indicative of the very slow change in perceptions about women's role and status which still exclusively depends on their fertility. No change is visible among the 15-29 age group of currently married women. No comparable statistics are available on the ever married group. Currently married women between 30-34 years do show marginal changes in their fertility behavior. Those figures indicate that family planning methods are adopted only after 3 to 4 births have taken place.

The age specific fertility rates calculated from census to census and the total fertility rate (TFR) do show significant changes in fertility behavior between 1981 and 1991 censuses (Table 2.9). It has declined from 6.3 to 5.7 per women in the fertile age group. Yet fertility has actually increased among 15 - 29 age group, which is very strange given a significant decline in the rate of early marriages between 1981 and 1991 and a perceptible increase in the literacy rate among the young women. (See chapter III below).

Table 2.9 Indicators of Fertility Behavior
(Number of Children Per Women)

| Age Group | Fertility Surveys | | Census to Census Estimatesc/ | | |
| | Currently Married | | All Women | | |
	1971 - 76a/	1991b/	1971	1981	1991
15 - 19	0.3	0.5	0.074	0.066	0.082
20 - 24	1.4	1.5	0.267	0.230	0.281
25 - 29	2.9	2.9	0.310	0.266	0.277
30 - 34	4.2	4.0	0.261	0.245	0.219
35 - 39	5.2	5.0	0.196	0.206	0.161
40 - 44	5.7	5.6	0.109	0.142	0.086
45 - 49	6.1	6.1	0.043	0.099	0.036
TMFR	6.1	6.1			
TFR			6.3	6.3	5.7

Source: a/ Nepal Fertility Survey, 1976, Table 5.1.

b/ Nepal Fertility, Family Planning & Health Survey, 1991, Table - 6.3.

c/ R.K. Gharty Chhetry, 1994, Table 1.

Fig 2.2 Total Marital Fertility Rate

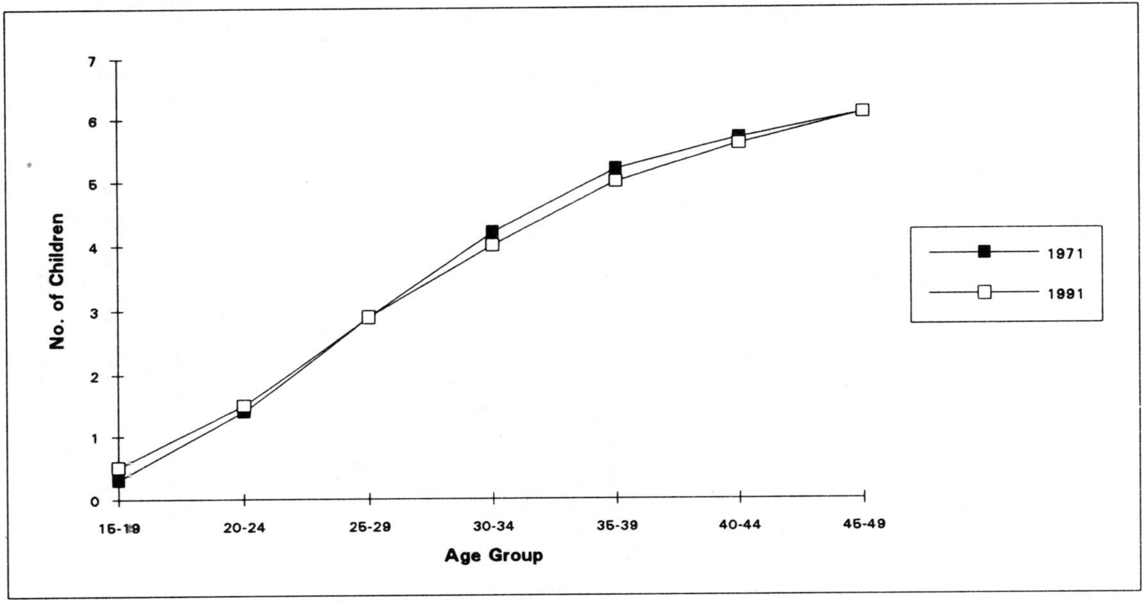

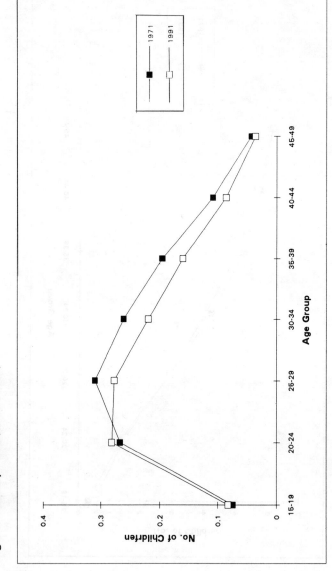

Fig 2.3 Fertility Rate (All Women)

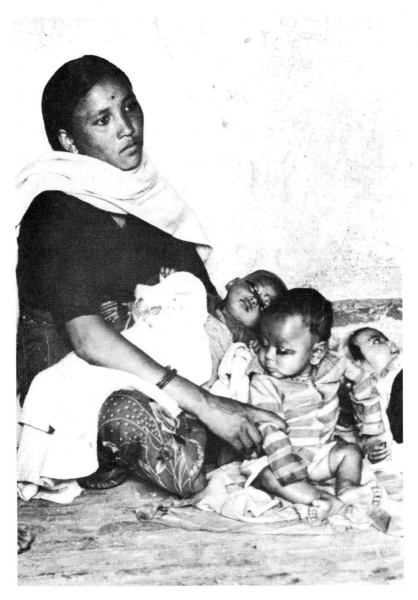

A long wait for vaccina

Table 2.10 Knowledge and Use of Contraceptics

(Percent of currently married women)

Year	Know at least one method	Current use (non-pregnant)
1976	21.3	3.9
1981	51.9	7.6
1986	55.9	15.1
1991	92.7	24.1

Source: NFHS, 1991 Table 9.2 & 9.9.

Although strictly comparable figures are not available, a comparison of children ever born and surviving to married women in 1991 in relation to similar indicators regarding ever married women in 1971-76, show that the rate of child survival has also improved notably, from 72.7 percent of births in 1971-76 to 82.9 percent in 1991 (Table 2.11).

Table 2.11 Mean Number of Children Ever Born and Children Still Alive

Age Group	1971 - 76 a/		1991 b/	
	To ever married women		To currently married women	
	Ever born	Still alive	Ever born	Still alive
15 - 19	0.3	0.3	0.5	0.4
20 - 24	1.4	1.1	1.5	1.4
25 - 29	2.9	2.3	2.9	2.5
30 - 34	4.1	3.1	4.0	3.4
35 - 39	5.1	3.7	5.0	4.0
40 - 44	5.5	3.8	5.6	4.5
45 - 49	5.7	4.0	6.1	4.7
All Total	3.3	2.4	3.5	2.9

Source: a/ Nepal Fertility Survey 1976, Table 5.9.
b/ NFHS, 1991 Table 6.3

There is a significant difference between the fertility behavior of urban and rural women. Urban women give birth to less children (5.3) during their life time than their rural sisters (6.2). The total marital fertility rate differs perceptibly also by education levels. Illiterate women have as much as 1.4 children more than those with some primary education (Table 2.12). Higher school education also makes a substantial difference.

Table 2.12 Some Indicators by Socio-Economic Group

Indicators	Residence			Education		
	Nepal	Rural	Urban	None	Primary	Secondary
Median Age of Marriage (20-49) Age Group	16.4	16.3	17.3	16.1	17.0	19.1
Knowledge of Contraception	92.6	72.9	90.1	91.7	97.8	99.7
TMFR	6.1	6.2	5.3	6.2	4.8	4.0
Birth Intervals (months)	33.7	33.8	32.7	34.2	31.2	27.8

Sources: NFHS, 1991 Various Tables.

These figures, however, should be considered holding income constant. Unfortunately, no data on fertility relating to income levels have been collected or analyzed. Low income groups do tend to have larger families compared to higher income families (Table 2.13). But it may not entirely be due to higher fertility of the poor women. Higher death rate among the poor women will also tend to increase the number of motherless children in the household and thus increase the number of children per surviving women. Higher infant mortality in these households compared to the non-poor ones, on the other hand, would have negative effect on the child/women ratio. No definite conclusions can be made from this data on the fertility of the poor women vs. non-poor women.

Table 2.13 Household Size & Child-Women Ratio By Income

Particulars	Poor		Not Poor	
	Hills	Tarai	Hills	Tarai
Rural				
1. Household Size a/	6.1	7.1	5.4	6.8
2. Number of children 10-14 per women between ages of 15-49	1.9	2.0	1.4	1.6
Urban				
1. Household size a/	6.3	6.9	5.1	5.5
2. Number of children 10-14 per women between ages of 15-49	2.1	2.2	2.1	1.2

Source: MPHBS, 1984 Special Tabulations.

a/ Average number of persons in the household per family.

Mountain families seem to have fertility rates much higher than the national average (Table 2.14). This may probably be explained by the lack of family planning services in mountain areas.

Table 2.14 Total Marital Fertility Rate by Region

| Region | Development Region | | | | | Regional |
	Eastern	Central	Western	Mid Western	Far Western	
Mountain	6.2	6.2	7.2	7.2	7.2	6.6
Hill	7.2	6.2	5.4	6.5	6.0	6.1
Tarai	5.7	5.8	6.6	6.5	6.5	6.0
Regional	6.2	5.9	5.8	6.5	6.5	6.1

Source: NFHS, 1991

2.5 Mortality and Life Expectancy

Infant and child mortality rates are important indicators of women's status. This is because while, on the one hand, infant and child mortality rates reflect social attitudes towards male and female children, on the other hand, they throw light on the situation of women as mothers. A comparatively higher female infant and child mortality rate signifies social neglect of female infants and children. At the same time, a high infant and child mortality rate force women to multiple and wasted pregnancies, thus depleting their strength.

Infant mortality rates (IMR) in Nepal, although declining over the years, are still one of the highest in the region. The Demographic Sample Survey of 1976 estimated the IMR at 132.5 per 1000. The NFHS Survey 1991 confirms the IMR at 98 with 104.7 for males and 91.0 for females (Table 2.15). This sex differential, if accurate, reverses the earlier trend with higher mortality for female infants.

As discussed earlier, it is a scientifically proven fact that female children are stronger than male children during their infancy and early childhood. As such, in the natural process more boys than girls are born. Given equal treatment, their ratios would equalize around 5 years of age. If a larger proportion of girls die during infancy and childhood it must therefore be due to social discrimination. A change in the ratio of male/female infant and child mortality rates towards approximating the natural phenomenon

Learning to make Nun-Chini-Pani.

may, therefore, be taken as an indicator of more equal social behavior towards female children. According to the figures for late seventies and 1991 NFHS Survey a lower proportion of girls are dying at infancy. That is compatible with the declining male/female sex ratio discussed earlier.

Table 2.15 Infant Mortality Rate (IMR)

(per 1000 live births)

Particulars	Year	Male	Female	Both Sex
DSS 1976a/	1974-75			
Urban	"	55.2	59.2	57.1
Rural	"	143.9	124.9	134.8
Total	"	141.2	123.0	132.5
DSS 1977b/	1976			
Urban	"	55.3	50.2	52.8
Rural	"	130.7	140.6	136.1
Total	"	128.4	137.9	133.6
NFS 1977c/	1976	--	--	152.0
DSS 1978d/	1977-78			
Urban	"	—	—	67.2
Rural	"	—	—	105.1
Total	"	110.0	98.0	104.0
CBS 1985e/	1978	147.0	142.0	144.0
New Era,1986f/	1981	136.0	111.0	117.0
NFFS 1986a/	1986	117.0	98.0	108.0
NFHS 1991g/	1990-91			
Urban	"	--	--	60.4
Rural	"	--	--	100.2
Total	"	104.7	91.0	98.0

Source: a/ CBS, 1976, The Demographic Sample Survey of Nepal, 1974-75, Survey Method and Findings, Kathmandu.

b/ CBS, 1977, The Demographic Sample Survey of Nepal, Second Year Survey, 1976, Kathmandu.

c/ Nepal FP/MCH Project 1977, Nepal Fertility Survey 1976, First Report, Kathmandu.

d/ CBS 1978, DSS of Nepal, Third Year Survey 1977-78, Kathmandu.

e/ CBS 1985, Inter-censal Changes of Some Key Census Variables, Nepal 1952/54 - 81.

f/ New Era 1986: Nepal Fertility & Mortality Survey - A Preliminary Report extracted from Population Monograph of Nepal, 1987.

g/ NFHS, 1991 Tables 10.3 and 10.4.

Nevertheless, as far as under five child mortality rates are concerned, the social discrimination against girls is clearly indicated by the child mortality rate figures. While only 125 per 1000 boys under five die annually, the number of girls dying before they are five year old is 139 per 1000. These figures are still one of the higher ones in the region (Table 2.16).

Table 2.16 Under Five Mortality Rate
by Sex in SAARC Countries, 1991

(Per Thousand Live Births)

SAARC Countries	1989a/		1991b/	
	Male	Female	Male	Female
Bangladesh	146	162	130	136
Bhutan	180	187	188	200
Nepal	178	187	125	139
India	118	134	123	125
Pakistan	145c/	151c/	137	139
Sri Lanka	28	22	25	19

Sources: a/ World Bank : World Development Report, 1991.

b/ World Bank : World Development Report, 1993.

c/ Figure are for 1990; World Bank, World Development Report 1992.

Similarly, the crude death rate (CDR) is one of the simplest and most common measures of mortality. Adult mortality rates are affected by nutritional status, both in early childhood and during adult life, access to food and health facilities and other environmental factors, such as pollution. In a country such as Nepal, where vital registration is not well established and information on deaths recorded in the national census is grossly under-reported, other indirect techniques are used to estimate death rates.

Estimates of CDR obtained from diverse sources differ. The most reliable estimates on the crude death rate were obtained from the 1985 CBS Survey in which direct information on deaths occurring during the two years preceding the survey was collected. There has been a substantial decline in the crude death rate during the last three decades. A 50 percent decline in the CDR is observed between 1953-61 and 1971-81 from 27.0 deaths per 1000 to 13.5 (Table 2.17). The Nepal Fertility and Mortality Survey, 1986 reported a still lower figure for 1984. The later estimates, however, show higher mortality rates. These have not been broken down on a gender basis.

Table 2.17 Estimates of Crude Death Rate

(per '000 population)

Particulars	Period of Estimation	Male	Female	Both sex
Tuladhar, Gubaju				
& Stoeckel, 1977a/	1961			22 - 27
	1971			22
DSS 1976b/	1974-75			
Urban	"	8.7	9.4	9.0
Rural	"	18.9	20.7	19.8
Total	"	18.6	20.4	19.5
DSS 1977c/	1976			
Urban	"	8.2	9.7	8.9
Rural	"	21.9	23.2	22.6
Total	"	21.5	22.8	22.2
DSS 1978d/	1977-78			
Urban	"	na	na	12.0
Rural	"	na	na	18.6
Total	"	17.9	16.2	17.1
CBS 1985e/	1971-81	12.2	14.9	13.5
New Era 1986f/	1984	10.8	11.0	10.9
CBS 1993g/	1991			16.4

a/   Tuladhar, Jayanti, Gubhaju, B.B., Stoeckel, John, 1977: "The Population of
      Nepal: Structure and Change; University of California Press, Berkeley.

b/   CBS, 1976, The Demographic Sample Survey of Nepal, 1974-75 Survey
      Methods and Findings, Kathmandu.

c/   CBS, 1977, The Demographic Sample Survey of Nepal, Second Year Survey
      1976, Kathmandu.

d/   CBS 1978, Demographic Sample Survey of Nepal, Third Year Survey 1977-78,
      Kathmandu.

e/   CBS 1985, Inter-censal Changes of Some Key Census Variables, Nepal 1952/
      54-81.

f/   New Era 1986, Fertility & Mortality Rates in Nepal - a Survey Report Submitted
      to National Commission on Population, Kathmandu.

g/   CBS, 1993, The Analysis of the 1991 Population Census (based on advance
      tables).

As indicated by these statistics, a higher proportion of women, as compared
to men, has been dying in Nepal. That is contrary to the international trend

which indicates higher mortality among men. The higher mortality of women in Nepal is attributed to a higher female child, and maternal mortality rates. For example, even within South Asia, Nepal was reported to have the highest maternal mortality rate at 850 per hundred thousand population (Table 2.18) in 1988. More recent survey NFHS (1991), however, reports substantially lower maternal mortality at 515 per 100,000 live births.

Table 2.18 Selected Demographic Indicators for SAARC Countries

Indicators	Nepal	Bangladesh	Bhutan	India	Pakistan	Sri Lanka
1. Infant Mortality$d$/ Rate per 1,000 live births						
Male	104.7a/	94e/	-	-	-	-
Female	91.0a/	87e/	-	-	-	-
Total	98.0a/	111	133	90	101	25
2. Crude Death Rates$b$/ Per 1000 population						
Male	12.2g/	12.3h/	-	-	-	7.3i/
Female	14.9g/	11.6h/	-	-	-	5.0i/
Total	13.0	13.0	17.0	10.0	11.0	6.0
3. Life Expectancy at birth (in years)b/						
Male	55.0c/	56.4e/	48	60	59	70
Female	53.0c/	55.4e/	50	61	59	74
Total	54.3c/	56.1f/	-	-	-	-
4. Maternal Mortality Rate per 100,000 live births 1988d/	850	650	800	550	600	180

Source : a/   Nepal Fertility and Family Planning Survey, 1991; Main Report

 b/   The World Bank World Development Report, 1993

 c/   CBS Estimates based on Population Census, 1991

 d/   UNDP, Human Development Report, 1993

 e/   Bangladesh Bureau of Statistics, Women and Men in Bangladesh, Facts & Figures, 1992

 f/   Provisional figures for 1991, Bangladesh Bureau of Statistics, Statistical Yearbook of Bangladesh, 1992

 g/   CBS, 1985, Inter-censal Changes of Some Key Census Variables, Nepal, 1952/54-81

 h/   Figures refer to 1986; United Nations Demographic Year Book, 1991

 i/   Figures refer to 1985.

As a consequence of such factors — higher infant and child mortality among female children and high maternal mortality rates- life expectancy at birth is lower for women than for men in Nepal (Table 2.19). However, with recent changes in infant mortality rates in favor of female children and a decline in the maternal mortality rate, women's life expectancy at birth may have improved significantly, though that has not, as yet, been reflected in estimates of current life expectancies.

Table 2.19: Life Expectancy at Birth

	Year	Male	Female
DSS 1976	1974 - 75	46.0	42.5
	1976	43.4	41.1
CBS 1986a/	1971 - 81	46.3	44.3
CBS 1986a/	1981	50.9	48.1
MOHb/	1990	55.4	52.6

Source: a/ CBS 1986 - Estimated Life-Tables of Nepal 1971-78 & 1981
       b/ MOH = Ministry of Health

III. SOCIAL CHARACTERISTICS

3.1 Marital Status

Marital options, i.e. the woman's say in deciding to get married, or not, to whom and when, are important indicators of her social status (see Giele, 1977). Marriage is the single most important event in the life of a woman since, in most societies, that still offer the only respected career opening for her. That event decides all her life options and subsequent livelihood. According to the Hindu tradition, marriage is a must for all, whether man or woman. While a man's life is not considered complete without a wife, a woman has no option but to get married. Hence, in Nepal, the overwhelming majority of both men and women are married before they are 25 years old. In 1991, 86.1 percent of women and 61.3 percent of men were married before that age. The corresponding percentages for women and men, in 1971, were 92.1 and 66.9 (Table 3.1). In the Indo-Aryan cultural groups, girls are married off by their parents in their early teens or even earlier. Since women are tied for life by their marriage bonds, their power to accept or reject such partnerships is evidently an index of the degree of freedom they exercise in the management of their own lives, and thus also of their status. In the case of early marriages, the concerned children are too young to comprehend the issues involved. By the time they wake up to reality, they are tied down for life. Early marriages are rooted to the concept of purity of the female body in the Indo-Aryan community (see Bennett, 1979) and to the need for helping hands in farm households (Acharya and Bennett, 1981). A decline in the mean age of marriage would indicate some relaxation in early marriage practices and of social control over female sexuality.

For women, the mean age at marriage has increased significantly from 15.4 years in 1961 to 18.0 years in 1991, indicating a slow but steady change in social perceptions about the institution of child marriage (Table 3.2). Between those two census years, the mean age of marriage increased by about 2 years for men and 2.7 years for women, on the average.

The change is most pronounced for young girls. In 1991, 7.4 percent of females in the 10-14 age group were reported to be already married as against 14.3 percent in 1981. In 1991, 86 percent of women in 20-24 age group were married. That compares well to the figure of 95 percent in 1961.

The proportion of the ever married population was lower in 1981 as compared to that indicated in the 1971 census in all but the 10-14 age group. That declining trend has been observed in the 1981-1991 decade in the 10-14 and 15-19 age groups (Table 3.2). Marriages of girl children before the age of 15 seem to be on decline. The proportion of girls who were married (married+widowed+divorced/separated) between 10-14 years has declined from 13.5 percent in 1971 to 7.4 percent in 1991.

Table 3.1 Mean Age at Marriage by Sex

(Age in years)

Year	Male	Female
1961a/	19.5	15.4
1971b/	20.9	16.8
1981c/	21.8	17.1
1991d/	21.4	18.1

Source: a/ The Analysis of Pop. Statistics of Nepal 1977.
b/ CBS 1987, DSS 1986/87 First Report pp. 55.
c/ CBS 1984, Population Census 1981; Vol.II Tab-5.
d/ CBS 1993, Population Census 1991.

Table 3.2 Age Specific Distribution of Ever Married Population by Sex

(As Percent of the Total Population of Respective Sex & Age Group)

Age Group	1961		1971		1981		1991	
	Male	Female	Male	Female	Male	Female	Male	Female
10 - 14	10.7	24.9	6.3	13.4	14.9	14.3	4.2	7.4
15 - 19	36.6	73.9	27.0	60.7	25.9	50.8	19.9	46.0
20 - 24	73.2	94.6	66.9	92.1	59.2	86.9	61.3	86.1
25 - 29	89.7	98.1	87.7	97.4	80.5	94.7	86.9	95.7
30 - 34	95.2	99.0	94.4	98.6	87.6	96.9	94.5	97.7
35 - 39	97.3	99.2	96.8	98.9	91.1	97.4	97.0	98.4
40 - 44	97.9	99.3	97.7	99.1	92.0	97.5	97.6	98.7
45 - 49	98.4	99.4	98.4	99.2	92.6	97.1	98.1	98.8
50 - 54	98.5	99.5	98.6	99.3	93.1	96.4	98.2	98.5
55 - 59	98.7	99.5	98.8	99.3	93.0	95.8	98.3	98.4
60 - 64	99.0	99.5	98.9	99.4	92.9	94.9	98.3	98.1
65 +	--	--	99.0	99.4	91.6	92.9	98.0	97.5
Average	65.4	69.2	64.1	70.3	62.1	70.8	64.0	73.6

Sources:- a/ The Analysis of the Pop. Statistics of Nepal 1977. Table 5.4
b/ Population Census 1981 and 1991.

Early widowhood with little possibility of remarriage is another curse upon women. Inter-censal comparison of divorce and seperation rates is rather difficult. That is because although each census provides information on marital status under four categories — never married, married, widowed

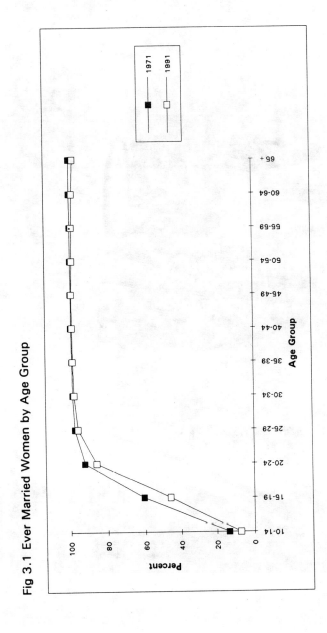

Fig 3.1 Ever Married Women by Age Group

31

Early marriage and work responsibilities.

and divorced/separated — there is a marked difference between the definitions employed by the census of 1961, 1971 and 1981 on the one hand by the definition employed by the 1991 census and on the other hand. The 1991 census has placed greater emphasis on legal aspects of marriage, while the former place more stress on religious and social dimensions. The following analysis should be considered bearing that in mind.

More than 1.6 percent of the female population — i.e. seven thousand women — were already widowed by 29 years of age. The risk of widowhood tends to increase with age. The percentage of widowed females in younger age groups, as well as in the total female population, is lower in 1991 as compared to that in 1971 — indicating a declining death rate of the male population. Between 1981 and 1991, however, the proportion of widowed female population has shown an increase. The divorces/ separated rate, on the other hand, has shown an increasing trend from 0.3 percent of the total population in 1971 to 0.4 and 0.7 percent in 1981 and 1991 respectively (Table 3.3). Divorce rates also increase with age. Even girls in the 10-14 age group face the risk of widowhood as well as of divorce. While a higher proportion of divorced women may indicate an increased determination to escape from oppressive marriages and situations of polygamy, it may also indicate increasing abandonment by men. Even today, women who are divorcees are stigmatized in the Hindu tradition. Thus, a divorcee has little chance of re-marriage within her own socio-economic group if she comes from a high/caste/class Hindu family. The need, from the religious point of view, to keep the clan's blood pure is a overwhelming factor in thus condemning women to single status for life or loss of social status, if her first marriage fails.

From the regional perspective, a higher proportion of females is married at an earlier age in the Tarai than in the Hills and Mountains. In 1991, more than 90 percent of the females in the Tarai were married by the time they had reached the age of 24. The corresponding figures were notably lower, standing at 82.4 percent for the Hills and 83.6 percent for the Mountains (Table 3.4). That difference has generally been maintained between the 1971 and 1991 census periods.

Table 3.3 Age Specific Marital Status of Female Population

(Row Percent)

Age Groups	Never Married			Currently Married			Widowed			Divorced/Separated		
	1971	1981	1991	1971	1981	1991	1971	1981	1991	1971	1981	1991
10 - 14	86.6	85.7	92.4	13.4	13.4	7.2	0.1	0.7	0.1	0.0	0.2	0.1
15 - 19	39.3	49.2	52.7	60.2	50.1	45.5	0.3	0.5	0.2	0.2	0.3	0.3
20 - 24	7.9	13.1	12.8	91.1	85.9	85.1	0.7	0.6	0.4	0.3	0.4	0.6
25 - 29	2.6	5,4	3.7	95.4	93.2	94.1	1.6	1.0	0.9	0.4	0.4	0.7
30 - 34	1.4	3.1	1.9	95.0	94.8	95.1	3.3	1.7	1.8	0.3	0.4	0.8
35 - 39	1.1	2.6	1.3	92.0	93.8	93.9	6.6	3.1	3.6	0.4	0.5	0.9
40 - 44	0.9	2.5	1.1	86.6	91.1	90.9	12.1	5.8	6.7	0.3	0.5	1.1
45 - 49	0.8	2.9	0.9	80.6	87.8	86.3	18.3	8.7	11.4	0.4	0.5	1.2
50 - 54	0.7	3.6	0.9	70.8	81.7	78.2	28.1	14.1	18.9	0.3	0.6	1.4
55 - 59	0.7	4.2	0.9	66.6	79.1	72.3	32.4	16.2	24.9	0.3	0.6	1.3
60 - 64	0.6	5.1	0.9	50.3	66.7	58.4	48.7	27.5	38.4	0.4	0.7	1.3
65 +	0.6	7.1	0.9	39.3	56.7	42.8	59.7	35,6	53.9	0.3	0.6	0.9
Total	**19.3**	**23.3**	**25.7**	**70.3**	**70.7**	**65.7**	**10.1**	**5.4**	**7.2**	**0.3**	**0.4**	**0.7**
Number	**(782)**	**(1,195)**	**(1,686)**	**(2,837)**	**(3,634)**	**(4,310)**	**(408)**	**(280)**	**(471)**	**(11)**	**(21)**	**(45)**

Source: Population Census, 1971, 1981 and 1991, CBS.
Note: i). Figures within the parentheses indicate number in thousand.
*   ii). Row total may not come to 100 as the percent under the "not stated"*
*   category is not included.*

The divorce/separated rate in the Mountains is higher than in the Hills or in the Tarai. The divorce rate in the Tarai is the lowest of all three regions, for all three censuses. Such figures may indicate that in the Tarai the forces of tradition exercise the maximum hold over women's lives. Among the Mountain population the Tibeto-Burman group dominates. These communities provide more life options to women where even divorcees may lead normal lives. In 1981, the widowhood rate was highest in the Tarai with 6.1 percent of the total female population widowed. In 1991, however, it shows up as highest in the Mountains, at 8.2 percent (Table 3.5). No consistent pattern has been observed between the three censuses regarding the proportion of widowed women in the three regions. It has declined between 1971 and 1981 in all three, but has increased, again in all three, in 1991. In the face of more rapidly declining death rates for men vis-a-vis women, it is difficult to fathom why a larger proportion of women were widowed in 1991, as compared to 1981.

Table 3.4 Proportion of Ever Married Population by Geographic Region, Age & Sex
(In percent to total Pop. in resp. age/sex)

Age Group	Mountain						Hills						Tarai					
	Male			Female			Male			Female			Male			Female		
	1971	1981	1991	1971	1981	1991	1971	1981	1991	1971	1981	1991	1971	1981	1991	1971	1981	1991
10 - 14	1.8	13.9	2.5	4.6	10.9	4.6	1.8	13.7	2.8	5.1	10.6	4.1	11.4	16.4	5.8	25.6	19.4	11.4
15 - 19	15.2	21.8	17.4	34.8	40.4	42.8	18.5	21.9	14.0	51.4	42.8	37.0	38.3	31.9	26.0	75.1	64.0	56.5
20 - 24	52.1	53.5	60.3	75.3	80.3	83.6	62.8	53.7	56.4	88.7	92.4	82.4	72.7	66.3	66.0	96.3	93.2	90.4
25 - 29	76.3	76.6	85.2	89.8	91.6	93.7	86.9	75.9	84.5	96.6	92.7	94.2	90.0	85.3	89.1	98.9	92.3	97.6
30 - 34	88.3	85.9	92.7	94.3	95.8	96.2	94.7	89.5	93.3	98.2	98.7	96.7	95.3	90.9	95.7	99.5	98.4	98.8
35 - 39	92.7	90.1	95.3	96.2	96.6	97.5	97.2	88.8	96.3	98.8	96.5	97.7	97.2	93.4	97.8	99.7	98.5	99.3
40 - 44	95.2	92.0	96.6	97.1	97.1	97.8	98.0	90.1	97.2	99.1	96.5	98.2	98.0	93.9	98.2	99.8	98.4	99.3
45 - 49	97.4	92.6	97.3	97.5	96.7	98.2	98.8	91.0	97.9	99.1	96.4	98.4	98.5	94.3	98.5	99.8	97.9	99.4
50 - 54	97.7	93.9	97.7	98.0	96.8	98.0	99.0	91.8	98.0	99.2	95.8	98.2	98.4	94.5	98.5	99.7	97.3	99.1
55 - 59	96.3	93.0	97.9	87.3	95.8	98.0	99.1	91.7	98.2	99.3	95.0	98.1	98.7	94.4	98.6	99.7	96.9	99.0
60 - 64	97.6	92.9	97.9	98.5	94.9	97.4	99.1	91.6	98.2	99.4	94.1	97.8	98.7	94.1	98.4	99.7	95.9	98.6
65 +	97.9	91.7	98.0	98.3	92.9	97.1	99.1	90.4	98.0	99.3	91.8	97.3	98.9	92.9	98.0	99.6	94.1	97.9
Total	51.4	63.9	63.9	63.3	74.5	72.8	54.9	61.3	60.9	66.9	73.3	70.2	62.7	68.9	66.8	74.4	81.2	77.3

Source: a/ The analysis of Population Statistics of Nepal 1977.
b/ Population Census - 1981 and 1991.

35

Table 3.5 Proportion of Divorced and Widowed Female Population by Geographic Region
(In percent to total female population in resp. age groups/regions)

(Row Percent)

Age Group	Mountain						Hills						Tarai					
	Widowed			Divorced/Seperated			Widowed			Divorced/Seperated			Widowed			Divorced/Seperated		
	1971	1981	1991	1971	1981	1991	1971	1981	1991	1971	1981	1991	1971	1981	1991	1971	1981	1991
10 - 14	0.1	0.1	0.1	--	0.2	0.1	0.03	0.6	0.04	0.01	0.3	0.1	0.1	0.8	0.1	0.02	0.2	0.1
15 - 19	0.2	0.1	0.2	0.1	0.2	0.4	0.3	0.5	0.1	0.2	0.3	0.4	0.3	0.5	0.2	0.1	0.3	0.3
20 - 24	0.8	0.7	0.5	0.5	0.6	0.9	0.7	0.6	0.4	0.5	0.5	0.7	0.4	0.6	0.4	0.2	0.3	0.5
25 - 29	2.0	1.2	1.1	0.5	0.7	1.0	1.7	1.0	0.9	0.5	0.5	0.9	1.5	1.1	0.9	0.2	0.3	0.5
30 - 34	3.6	2.0	2.2	0.6	0.6	1.1	3.5	1.7	1.8	0.4	0.5	1.0	3.0	1.8	1.6	0.2	0.3	0.6
35 - 39	5.9	3.3	4.5	0.6	0.6	1.2	7.0	2.6	3.5	0.4	0.5	1.1	6.4	3.5	3.6	0.2	0.3	0.7
40 - 44	10.4	6.2	8.6	0.7	0.8	1.5	12.8	5.1	6.8	0.3	0.6	1.3	12.2	6.5	6.4	0.3	0.4	0.7
45 - 49	13.3	8.2	13.4	0.5	0.8	1.3	16.7	7.5	10.9	0.3	0.6	1.4	20.3	10.4	11.5	0.2	0.4	0.9
50 - 54	21.4	12.7	20.8	0.4	0.7	1.4	26.6	11.8	18.0	0.3	0.7	1.7	31.9	17.7	19.6	0.2	0.5	1.0
55 - 59	24.4	14.1	26.6	0.6	0.6	1.5	30.7	14.9	24.5	0.2	0.6	1.6	35.7	18.3	24.9	0.2	0.5	0.9
60 - 64	36.5	24.4	39.3	0.3	0.6	1.4	47.1	23.1	35.8	0.4	0.7	1.5	56.6	33.9	41.2	0.2	0.7	1.0
65 +	48.3	32.0	52.5	0.3	0.7	0.9	56.3	31.3	52.2	0.2	0.7	1.0	66.7	42.0	56.2	0.2	0.6	0.7
Total	**8.0**	**5.3**	**8.2**	**0.4**	**0.5**	**0.9**	**8.7**	**4.9**	**7.2**	**0.3**	**0.5**	**0.8**	**9.2**	**6.1**	**7.0**	**0.1**	**0.3**	**0.5**

Source: Population Census, 1971, 1981 and 1991, CBS.

3.2 Education

Literacy and educational qualification are other vital indicators of women's social status. These are crucial factors for not only availing of employment opportunities created in the process of modernization but also for communication with the outside world as with increasingly educated males within the household. An educated wife and mother naturally has better communication with her educated male counterparts in the family and commands greater respect than one without education. Hence in addition to marriage options, educational attainment has become a most valuable indicator of a women's social status.

Nepal has made substantial progress in the field of education, during the past three decades. The overall literacy rate went up to 23.3 percent in 1981 and to 39.3 percent in 1991, as against about 13.9 percent in 1971 (Table 3.6). The male literacy rate has increased from 23.6 percent in 1971 to 34 percent in 1981 and 54 percent in 1991. The proportion of literate females is continuously moving up from 3.9 percent in 1971 to 12.1 percent in 1981 and 24.7 percent in 1991. However, the sex differential in the literacy rate is still high. The current female literacy rate is close to male literacy 20 years ago. The disparity between male and female educational attainments has not declined during the 1981-1991 decade. The difference between the male and female literacy rates, for example, has increased to about 29 percentage points in 1991 compared to about 20 percentage points in 1971 and about 22 percentage points in 1981. For every one hundred boys, only 53 girls receive primary school education.

Table 3.6 Literacy Rates
(As percent to the total population of six years and above)

Census	Male	Female	Both	Male/Female Differentials
1971	23.59	3.91	13.89	19.68
1981	33.96	12.05	23.26	21.91
1991	54.10	24.73	39.34	29.37

Source: Population Census, 1971, 1981 and 1991, CBS.

Age specific literacy rates also do not indicate very positive trend (Table 3.7). Even among the 15-19 age group the disparity in the proportion of literate men and women is increasing. For example while in 1981, the percentage point difference in the male and female literacy rate was 30.7 (48.2-17.5), in 1991 it had gone up to 32.8 (71.2-38.4). Only the 10-14 age group girls have started to catch up with same age cohort boys and the gender disparity in literacy rates has started to decline, e.g., from 29.6 percentage points in 1981 to 26.7 percentage points in 1991.

Table 3.7 Literacy Rates by Age Group and Sex
(In Percent to Population Age Group)

Age Group	1961 Male	1961 Female	1971 Male	1971 Female	1981 Male	1981 Female	1991 Male	1991 Female
10-14	14.5	3.1	35.8	9.6	50.8	21.2	75.8	49.1
15-19	19.5	2.4	35.4	7.1	48.2	17.5	71.2	38.4
20-24	20.2	1.6	30.9	4.1	41.7	12.6	64.0	26.1
25-29	17.4	1.2	24.4	2.5	36.3	10.1	54.4	17.5
30-34	16.4	1.2	20.3	1.6	31.8	7.8	49.4	13.8
35-39	16.4	0.9	17.6	1.4	27.6	6.7	45.0	11.1
40-44	15.4	0.9	16.4	1.1	23.7	5.5	40.9	7.8
45-54	14.3	0.8	15.7	1.0	17.3	4.8	19.9	3.4
55 +	13.0	0.6	12.6	0.7	19.1	4.0	11.9	1.8

Source: a/ Population Monograph of Nepal, CBS, 1987, Table 6.2.
          b/ Population Census, CBS, 1991.

The picture, according to the census data is not changing fast to a more positive educational status of girl children. Figures on enrollment levels obtained from the 1991 census paint a bleaker picture on the education front (Table 3.8). According to those figures, only 36.5 percent of children and 28.8 percent of girls in the 6-10 age group are going to school. There however seems to an inconsistency with respect to those figures. It seems that the questions regarding literacy of children were asked before those on enrollment and literate and beginners were listed as enrolled. A child just starting school can, after all, hardly be expected to be literate. The figures in Table 3.8 include literate and beginners at school. It probably under-estimates enrollment levels.

Table 3.8 Male/Female School Enrollment Level by Age Group and Region

Gender/Age Group	Percent of Age Cohort Mountain	Hills	Tarai	Nepal
Male (6-15)	53.0	59.4	39.4	57.7
6-10	44.3	48.6	39.7	43.9
11-15	63.3	71.6	60.5	66.0
Female (6-15)	24.8	38.9	29.5	33.6
6-10	22.7	34.6	24.5	28.8
11-15	27.2	43.9	37.0	39.7
Both Sexes (6-15)	39.1	49.3	39.4	43.9
6-10	33.7	41.7	32.3	36.5
11-15	45.7	57.9	49.5	53.3

Source: CBS 1994, Population Census 1991.

Fig 3.2 Male/Female Literacy Rate
Difference by Age Group

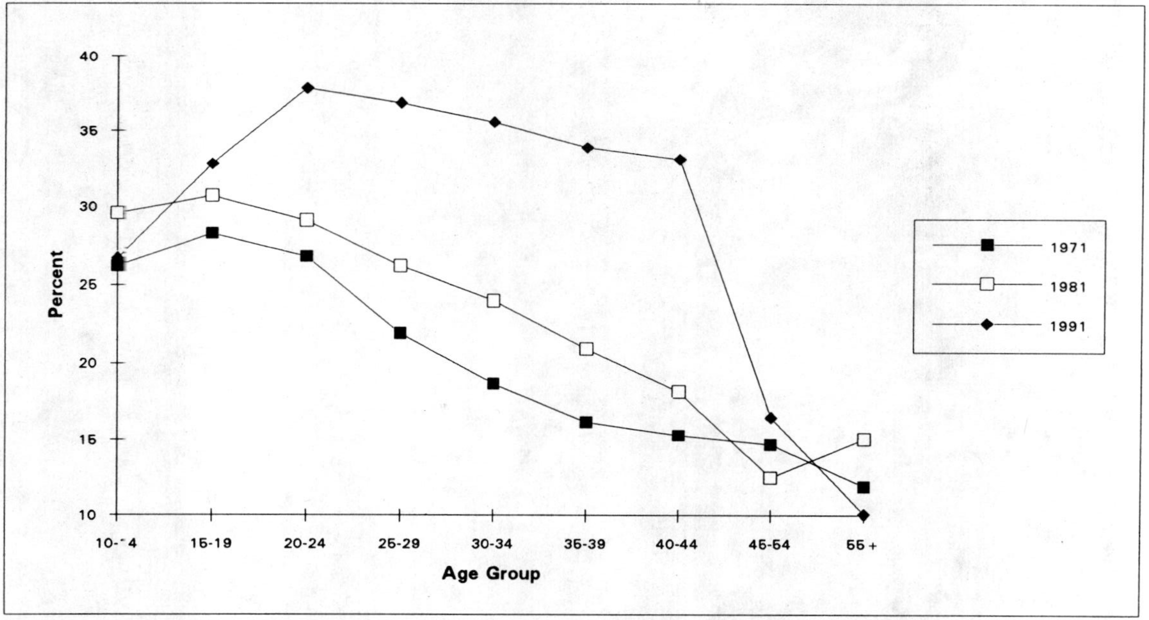

Making tea - The mountain way.

As the level of education increases, the ratio of females declines progressively. At the post-graduate level, the female-male ratio is less than one-to-four (Table 3.9).

Table 3.9 Some Indicators of Educational Attainment (for 6 years & above)

(Number in '000)

Particulars	1971			1981			1991		
	Male	Female	Females per 100 Males	Male	Female	Females per 100 Males	Male	Female	Females per 100 Males
Illiterate	3661.2	4480.0	122.4	4115.9	5230.3	127.1	3402.3	5671.1	166.7
Literate	1130.2	182.5	16.2	2117.0	716.4	33.8	4073.2	1885.5	46.3
a) No Schooling	--	--	--	506.9	163.3	32.2	906.9	453.4	50.0
b) Primary	131.2	13.6	10.4	975.6	404.4	41.5	1593.2	852.7	53.5
c) Lower Secondary	--	--	--	203.6	56.9	27.9	--	--	--
d) Secondary	--	--	--	267.6	57.3	21.4	966.6	378.9	39.2
e) SLC	55.5	6.5	11.7	76.6	17.0	22.2	229.0	71.3	31.2
f) Intermediate	--	--	--	46.6	10.0	21.5	107.8	28.4	26.4
g) Graduates	12.8	1.3	10.2	31.5	5.9	18.7	64.5	14.3	22.2
h) Post Graduates	--	--	--	9.2	1.6	17.6	14.7	3.5	23.7

Source: Population Census, 1971, 1981 and 1991, CBS.

Among the five development regions, the Western Development Region has the highest proportion of literate women — at 30.6 percent in 1991. The Mid-Western and Far-Western Development Regions lag far behind that level. On further classification, the Western Hill region tops the list with more than 34 percent literate women. The mountains of the Mid-Western Development Region with only 6.3 percent of women being able to read and write, is at the bottom of the literacy ladder. Similarly for males the highest literacy rate of 63.3 percent has been noted in the hills of the Western Development Region and the lowest of 36.6 percent in the Mid-Western Mountains (Table 3.10). The difference between male, female literacy rates is highest in the Far-Western Hills and Mountains. This indicates that discrimination against women is most acute in that region, dominated by Indo-Aryan cultural groups.

Table 3.10 Literacy Rates by Region

(As percent to the population of six years and above)

Development Region	Male			Female			Male/Female Differentials
	1971	1981	1991	1971	1981	1991	1991
Eastern	25.5	39.5	59.0	4.7	14.5	29.1	29.9
Mountain	23.5	40.6	61.7	3.2	12.1	28.7	33.0
Hills	23.9	38.7	61.0	3.2	11.7	28.2	32.8
Tarai	27.1	16.8	57.7	6.3	39.7	29.6	28.1
Central	23.1	32.3	51.6	4.8	12.5	24.4	27.2
Mountain	15.6	23.6	46.0	1.7	6.9	15.4	30.6
Hills	27.9	39.3	62.6	6.9	17.1	33.3	29.3
Tarai	19.9	27.5	42.7	3.4	9.3	17.6	25.1
Western	29.5	38.4	58.2	3.9	20.3	30.6	27.6
Mountain	19.5	31.4	59.1	5.0	12.4	33.4	25.7
Hills	31.7	41.3	63.3	3.8	14.1	34.4	28.9
Tarai	24.0	32.2	49.6	4.3	11.0	22.8	26.8
Mid West.*		25.3	47.4		7.3	16.1	31.3
Mountain		19.3	36.6		4.7	6.3	33.3
Hills		25.8	49.2		6.6	14.5	34.7
Tarai		26.5	48.1		9.3	21.1	27.0
Far West	16.3	26.8	51.6	1.6	7.7	13.1	38.5
Mountain	14.8	24.9	52.7	1.4	6.2	10.4	42.3
Hills	17.2	26.9	52.7	1.2	7.6	10.0	42.7
Tarai	15.1	28.0	50.0	3.1	8.7	18.0	32.0
All Nepal	**23.6**	**34.0**	**54.2**	**3.9**	**12.1**	**24.7**	**29.5**
Rural	**22.9**	**32.9**	**53.4**	**2.7**	**9.8**	**20.4**	**33.0**
Urban	**61.6**	**62.0**	**80.0**	**26.4**	**37.5**	**51.2**	**28.8**
Mountain	**17.6**	**27.6**	**49.8**	**2.1**	**7.8**	**16.3**	**33.5**
Hills	**25.8**	**36.9**	**59.9**	**3.9**	**12.9**	**28.3**	**31.6**
Tarai	**22.1**	**32.1**	**49.5**	**4.4**	**11.9**	**22.6**	**26.9**

Source: Population Census, 1971, 1981 and 1991, CBS.
* *This region was part of Western Development Region in 1971.*

Household income workload and the concern with the purity of the female body leading to the early marriage are important variables in female education. As long as there is no resource crunch in the family, the primary school age girls may get to go to school. But as soon as the resource constraint arises, the first casualty is the female child's education. Tables 3.11 and 3.12 clearly show that girls in lower income groups get fewer opportunities to go to school. Those who do go to school get little opportunity to further their education beyond the secondary level (Table 3.12).

Table 3.11 Primary School Enrollment Levels by Income Group

(In percent)

	Poor		Not Poor	
	Male	Female	Male	Female
Rural				
Hills	71.5	32.6	78.5	54.1
Tarai	45.0	13.9	67.1	39.2
Urban				
Hills	74.6	50.0	83.3	75.2
Tarai	48.6	26.4	72.0	50.9

Source: MPHBS Special Tabulations in Acharya, 1990.

Table 3.12 Level of Education by Income Group

(In Percent)

	Poor			Not Poor		
	Literate	Secondary	Higher	Literate	Secondary	Higher
			Rural			
Female						
Hills	19.1	2.3	0.0	28.6	5.9	0.0
Tarai	7.1	1.3	0.0	21.9	5.7	0.0
Male						
Hills	62.1	11.8	0.8	74.6	23.9	2.4
Tarai	37.3	8.5	0.4	57.0	19.2	3.1
			Urban			
Female						
Hills	25.7	4.6	0.0	57.4	4.6	5.9
Tarai	16.9	2.5	0.3	42.4	2.5	2.0
Male						
Hills	72.0	18.9	1.6	87.9	32.3	17.8
Tarai	53.1	14.9	1.3	73.3	26.1	9.4

Source: MPHBS Special Tabulations in Acharya, 1990.

Girls in the 6-9 age group have been reported to be working 2.6 to 4.5 hours per day compared to boys' 1.7 to 2.9 hours of work per day (Table 3.13). In rural areas, girls in 10-14 age groups work only slightly less hours when compared to the adult men.

Table 3.13: Time Use Pattern of Rural and Urban Children

(Hours per day)

Regions	Total Work -burden a/			
	Male		Female	
	Rural	Urban	Rural	Urban
Mountains b/				
15 and above	8.7	-	11.2	-
10 - 14 Years	4.4	-	7.7	-
6 - 9 Years	2.9	-	4.5	-
Hills				
15 and above	7.9	7.1	10.6	8.8
10 - 14 Years	4.1	1.6	7.0	4.0
6 - 9 Years	1.9	0.8	3.4	1.4
Tarai				
15 and above	7.8	7.8	9.4	8.9
10 - 14 Years	3.3	2.4	5.9	4.3
6 - 9 Years	1.7	1.0	2.6	2.2

Source: Multipurpose Household Budget Survey, Nepal Rastra Bank, p. 141-142, 1988.
a/   Includes domestic work and childcare, besides economic and subsistence economic activities. For detailed definition see Annex A.
b/   Mountains have no urban areas.

Another compelling factor hindering women's education in general is the fact that girls are transferred to her affinal households after marriage and consequently parents have no claim on her work or income as adult women. When parents are asked in various surveys as to why they are not sending their girl children to school one of the often repeated answer is "they will go to other people's house (Arkako Ghara Zane) so what is the use of educating them " (CERID, 1986 a and b). In summary, poverty, workload and cultural perceptions remain the major factors hindering female education.

Fig 3.3 Male Total Work Hours as Percent of Female Total Work Hours

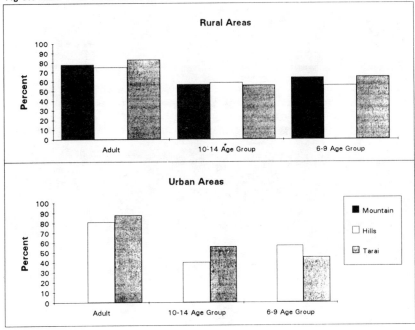

Rural Areas 3-5

Urban Areas

IV. ECONOMIC CHARACTERISTICS

4.1 Economic Activity Rates

Accuracy of reporting on labor force participation rates in censuses and the definition of economic activity are some of the major issues which concern women's rights activists the world over. Many books and reports have focussed on them. Several UN agencies have documented them in detail. (For example see Beneria, 1982 and UN, 1987). In Nepal, they have been detailed in *The Status of Women* in Nepal series. For example, Acharya (1979), after a discussion on the practical difficulties involved in defining women's gainful employment and the conceptual inadequacies of the very idea of economic activity itself, recommended that women should be classified into the three following groups in population censuses — (a) who produce marketable goods; (b) who are engaged in subsistence activities; and (c) who perform only domestic chores — in lieu of the present two categories, viz. "active" and "inactive." Yet 1981 and 1991 censuses continue to provide data on occupational distribution classified only into economically active and inactive.

The 1971 census defined economically active individuals as those who were either engaged in "gainful" employment for at least three months in the preceding year and who sought employment. The query of whether a person "worked" or not preceded questions related to the type or length of work involved. Under such a scheme the reported economic activity rates were high (82.9) for men and low (35.2) for women.

According to the 1981 census "the economic activity of a person" refers to gainful activity during a minimum eight-month period of the year preceding the census. If a person fulfilled such a requirement, the person's occupation, industry and employment status (i.e. whether as an employer or employee, own account worker or unpaid family worker) had to be declared. Those seeking work for the first time or who had worked for less than eight months were classified as "inactive." This census continued to show significant disparity between men's and women's economic activity rates (Table 4.1).

Table 4.1 Age Specific Participation Rates by Sex

Table 4.1 Age Specific Participation Rates by Sex
(In percent to total Pop. in respective sex & age group)

Age Group	Total			Male			Female		
	1971	1981	1991	1971	1981	1991	1971	1981	1991
10 - 14	50.5	56.9	22.9	59.2	61.3	18.1	40.1	51.9	28.0
15 - 19	61.6	60.7	49.1	75.7	69.2	49.2	46.2	51.3	49.0
20 - 24	63.5	66.1	66.0	89.8	86.3	80.0	39.2	47.6	54.1
25 - 29	65.3	68.7	72.0	95.1	93.4	92.3	36.6	44.9	53.9
30 - 34	63.7	68.2	73.6	96.6	95.3	95.2	33.9	43.3	53.8
35 - 39	66.9	70.8	75.3	97.4	95.8	95.9	34.0	44.1	54.5
40 - 44	64.7	70.4	74.3	97.2	96.0	95.5	32.9	44.1	54.1
45 - 49	66.7	72.3	73.8	96.8	96.4	94.7	32.5	44.7	52.1
50 - 54	62.9	71.2	70.4	94.0	94.3	91.7	30.5	44.0	48.0
55 - 59	60.0	69.9	66.6	93.3	92.2	88.2	27.7	43.3	41.5
60 - 64	39.7	62.5	45.7	64.1	83.3	66.2	17.9	39.9	25.4
65 +	25.1	52.9	26.7	40.5	68.7	40.0	10.4	35.0	12.8
Total	**59.3**	**65.1**	**56.6**	**82.9**	**83.2**	**68.2**	**35.2**	**46.2**	**45.2**

Source: Population Census, 1971, 1981 and 1991, CBS.

The Multi-purpose Household Budget Survey (MHBS) conducted by the
Nepal Rastra Bank in 1984/85, where no question about work preceded
those relating to duration and type of work, much higher economic activity
rates for women (69.9 percent) and much lower for men (76.1 percent) were
reported (NRB, MPHBS p. 192). It reported high total work load and
working hours for women (Table 4.2). It is probable that such an experience
influenced the 1991 questionnaires.

Table 4.2 Hours of Work Per Person Per Day (15 Years and Above)

Sex / Activities a/	Rural			Urban	
	Mountain	Hill	Tarai	Hill	Tarai
Male					
1) Conventional Economic	4.70	4.21	5.10	5.19	5.90
2) Subsistence Economic	1.80	1.61	0.95	0.41	0.34
Total Economic (1 + 2)	6.50	5.82	6.05	5.60	6.24
3) Domestic	2.19	2.07	1.79	1.41	1.59
Total (1+2+3)	8.69	7.89	7.84	7.01	7.83
Female					
1) Conventional Economic	3.57	2.68	1.70	1.70	1.32
2) Subsistence Economic	2.43	2.54	1.86	1.27	1.10
Total Economic (1 + 2)	6.0	5.22	3.56	2.97	2.42
3) Domestic	5.23	5.39	5.84	5.61	6.48
Total (1+2+3)	11.23	10.69	9.40	8.78	8.98

Source: MPHBS. 1984/85. NRB, 1988. P. 141
a) For definiton of the classification see Annex A.

Note: Mountains have no urban areas.

Fig. 4.1 Age Specific Participation Rates by Sex
(In percent to total Pop. in respective sex & age group)

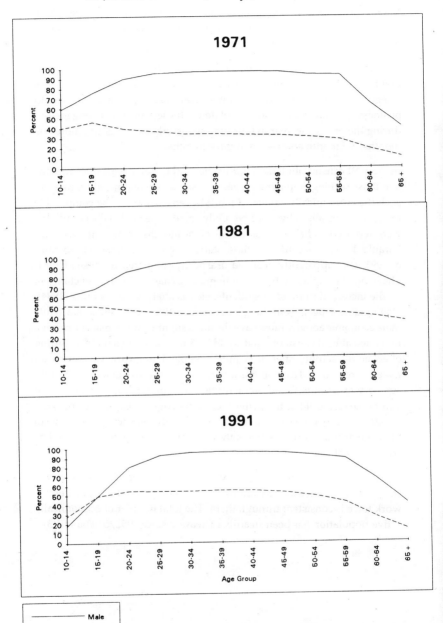

In 1991 census, people were first questioned about type of work done during the past 12 months, without prefacing that with a query regarding whether they worked at all, or not.

The type of work was classified in three categories while a fourth group identified those who did not work at all for pay or profit. The work categories were "agriculture", "wage/salary earnings" and "household business". The next question was related to the length of work engaged-in during the preceding year in four time spans: eight months and more, 6-7 months, 3-5 month and less than three months.

In the 1991 census tabulation, those who worked for at least three months and those seeking employment were classified as economically active. As such the economically actives of the 1981 census may not be comparable to the economically actives of 1991. Only about 38 percent of the population were reported as having worked for eight months or more in 1991 (see Niraula; 1994 a.) According to those statistics, gross economic activity rates of 1991 have apparently declined drastically compared to those of 1981. That could be explained by the demographic changes in favor of children, by the increased number of students, etc., as analyzed by Niraula (1994). One notable aspect, from the gender perspective, however, is that while male economic activity rates have declined significantly, female rates have remained almost constant. That could be due to a more accurate recording of economic activity rates. It is quite possible that in earlier censuses, all males were recorded as economically active, irrespective of length of work, age or work status while women were recorded as home makers. An additional fact could be that while most school-age male children are going to school, and were recorded as such, since only very few girls in the 10 plus age group study in schools they might not have been perceived as students at all.

Having noted such an inadequacy, we have proceeded to analyze the censuses' labor force data assuming that under-enumeration of the female work force is consistent through them. The total number of economically active population has been steadily increasing since 1952/54 (Table 4.3).

Table 4.3 Economically Active Population of 10 years and above by Sex

(Number in '000)

Sex	1952/54 a/		1961 a/		1971 a/		1981 b/		1991 b/	
	Number	Percent	Number	Percent	Number	Percent	Number	Percent	Number	Percent
Male	2,460	59.2	2,564	59.5	3,434	70.8	4,479	65.4	4375	59.6
Female	1,693	40.8	1,743	40.5	1,418	29.2	2,371	34.6	2964	40.4
Total	4,153	100.0	4,307	100.0	4,852	100.0	6,850	100.0	7339	100.0

Source: a/   The Status of Women in Nepal, Statistical Profile of Nepalese
             Women : A Critical review, Center for Economic
             Development and Administration, Kathmandu, 1979.
         b/   Population Census, 1981 and 1991, CBS.

The patterns of age-specific participation rates for males and females are significantly different. The activity rates for males increase steeply with age up to the 30-34 age group and remain almost constant at a high level of over 95 percent to the age of 45, after which they begin to fall. Women become economically active earlier. In the 1991 census, 28 percent of girls in the 10-14 age group were reported as economically active as compared to only 18 percent for boys in the same age group. The rate increases with age up to about the late forties, before it begins to decline. That pattern is considerably at variance with that reported in the 1981 census where the highest economic activity rates were reported for young women up to the age of 19 (Table 4.1).

With evidently inadequate data to reflect accurately the status of the working population, Acharya (1979)employed the concept of potential labor force for evaluating the male/female composition of the working population. The population in the 15-59 age group were defined as constituting the potential labor force. For the current analysis, that definition has been somewhat refined to include economically active home makers and students while excluding the physically sick and invalids. That seems quite in order since in Nepal more than 71[1] percent of household income is derived from production within the family farm and non-farm enterprises (MPHBS, 1989, P. 82). Women put in a larger proportion of labor in such enterprises (Acharya and Bennett, 1981). Furthermore, as students are also

---

1   Includes Agricultural and Non-Agricultural Enterprise plus goods produced at
     home and received free.

an integral part of the country's future labor force, they have been included in that category. However, students presently included in that definition are those in the 10-plus group because many children begin working on the farms and service sectors early in life. In other words, such working children do constitute a part of the working labor force. Women constitute slightly more than half of that potential labor force (Table 4.4).

Table 4.4 Potential Labor Force, 10 Years and Above
(Census Year 1971, 1991)

(In '000)

Census Year	Economically Active (a)		Home Maker (b)		Student (c)		Potential Labor Force (a+b+c)	
	Male	Female	Male	Female	Male	Female	Male	Female
1971	3,434	1,418	-	2,306	357	67	3,791	3,791
1981	4,480	2,371	7	2,260	591	221	5,078	4,852
1991	4,376	2,964	239	2,366	1,312	698	5,927	6,027

Source: Population Census, 1971, 1981 and 1991, CBS.

The daily chores of family life in rural Nepal involve women in labor-intensive farm work and time consuming domestic work to provide fuel, water and food for household members and farm workers. The census definition of economic activity in theory takes into account wage labor, in cash or kind, as well as unpaid family labor. It does not, however, encompass activities such as water and fuel collection, food processing and child care all of which are primarily the responsibility of women. Those activities that fall outside the formal economy, but which are essential for the survival of the household, absorb the labor of those women who are reported as "economically inactive" and classified as homemakers and dependents. As per the 1991 census data, more than 36 percent of the female population were reported as homemakers (Table 4.5) and so inactive.

A scrutiny of the regional figures clearly indicates a persisting reporting bias in economic activity rates. While the overwhelming majority of Mountain (73.6 percent) and Hill (57.9 percent) women are reported as economically active, only about 27 percent of the Tarai women are thus reported. *The Status of Women* report series had shown that women in the Tarai were equally active in the economic sphere, albeit invisibly, within the household production system e.g. in food processing and cooking for farm labor. (see Acharya, 1979).

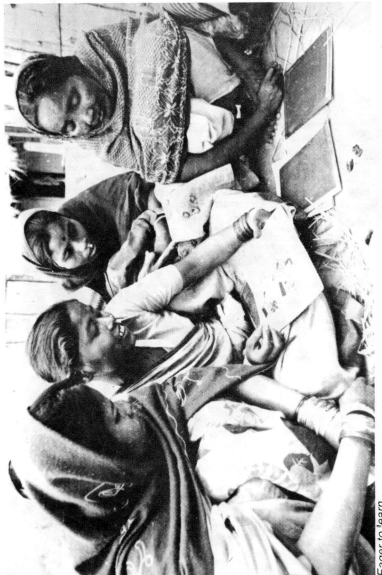

Eager to learn.

Water collection. - Universally women's responsibility.

Table 4.5 Economically Active Females & Housewives (Homemakers) of 10 years & above by region

(In Percent)

Regions/ Particulars	Eastern		Central		Western		Mid.Western		Far Western		Regional	
	1971	1991	1971	1991	1971	1991	1971	1991	1971	1991	1971	1991
Mountain												
Econ. Active	-	66.3	-	73.8	-	65.3	-	82.0	-	75.6	-	73.6
Home Makers	-	12.8	-	12.9	-	14.5	-	9.5	-	13.1	-	12.4
Hills												
Econ. Active	39.1	61.5	55.6	48.0	58.4	59.3	-	61.4	41.2	78.0	49.0	57.9
Home Makers	53.2	18.7	38.3	30.5	33.5	17.5	-	26.0	53.3	11.0	44.2	22.5
Tarai												
Econ. Active	16.9	28.3	6.6	19.4	22.4	35.2	-	31.6	15.6	32.2	13.4	26.9
Home Makers	74.3	49.5	85.9	64.3	69.1	46.4	-	51.0	77.6	52.0	78.5	54.5
All Nepal												
Econ. Active	28.6	42.3	28.6	36.5	50.2	51.4	-	52.4	36.8	60.2	35.1	45.2
Home Makers	63.1	36.4	63.0	45.1	41.6	27.0	-	33.7	57.5	26.9	57.1	36.1

Sources: i). Acharya, 1979 for 1971 figures.
ii). Population Census, 1991, CBS.

4.2 Industrial and Occupational Classification

Agriculture still predominates as a source of employment, although the share of the non-agriculture sector in total employment has shown a substantial increase in 1991 (Table 4.6). In 1981, more than 91 percent of the economically active population was involved in agriculture and forestry. The percentage of the economically active population in agriculture has decreased from 94.4 percent in 1971 to 91.2 percent in 1981 and further to 81.2 percent in 1991 (Table 4.7). Thus the decline in proportion of people in the agriculture sector is more pronounced in the 1991 census.

Table 4.6 Agriculture and Non-Agricultural Population
by Sex (10 years and above)

(In '000)

	1952/54	1961	1971	1981	1991
Agriculture					
Male	2,261	2,351	3,187	3,974	3,279
Female	1,629	1,688	1,392	2,270	2,683
Total	**3,890**	**4,039**	**4,579**	**6,244**	**5,962**
Non-Agriculture					
Male	199	190	247	506a/	1,097b/
Female	64	43	26	101	281
Total	**263**	**233**	**273**	**607**	**1,378**

Sources: i). Acharya, 1979 for 1971 figures.
ii). Population Census, 1991, CBS.
a/ includes category of 'not stated'.
b/ includes categories of 'others & not stated'.

Concomitantly there has been an increase in the proportion of the economically active population in the non-agriculture sector. The proportion of the men employed in the non-agriculture sector has increased from 7.2 percent in 1971 to 23.8 percent in 1991. Similarly, the corresponding figure for women increased from 1.8 percent in 1971 to 8.9 in 1991. In the non-agriculture sector, personnel and community services are the leading sources of employment for both men and women. According to the 1991 census, manufacturing is employing only 2 percent of the labor force — which is strange given the increase in industrial production and export in the past two decades. Even the survey of the manufacturing sector in 1990/91 reported about 160,000 workers only. According to the same survey, the value added in the manufacturing sector, on the other hand, has more than trebled between 1981/82 and 1990/91. The export of manufactured goods (SIT Categories 6 to 8) has increased from Rs. 399 million in 1980/81 to Rs. 5858 million in 1990/91 (NRB Quarterly Bulletin, Mid-October 1992). Such inconsistencies are difficult to explain. Commerce is generating employment for 3.5 percent which is higher by 1.5 percentage points than in manufacturing (Table 4.7).

Women are the backbone of the nepalese agriculture.

Table 4.7 Distribution of Economically Active Population by Industry

(In percent to total economically active pop.)

(In percent)

Industry	Total			Male			Female		
	1971	1981	1991	1971	1981	1991	1971	1981	1991
I. Agriculture & Forestry	94.4	91.2	81.2	92.8	88.7	74.9	98.2	95.8	90.5
II. Non-Agriculture	5.6	7.0	17.8	7.2	9.2	23.8	1.8	2.9	8.9
Manufacturing	1.1	0.5	2.0	1.3	0.6	2.6	0.5	0.2	1.2
Elect. Gas & Water	0.0	0.0	0.2	0.1	0.1	0.3	--	0.0	0.0
Construction	0.1	0.0	0.5	0.1	0.0	0.7	0.0	0.0	0.1
Commerce	1.3	1.6	3.5	1.6	2.1	4.5	0.6	0.7	2.0
Transport & Communication	0.2	0.1	0.7	0.3	0.2	1.1	0.0	0.0	0.1
Finance & Business Services	0.1	0.1	0.3	0.1	0.2	0.4	0.0	0.0	0.1
Personal & Community Services	2.8	4.6	10.3	3.7	6.0	13.6	0.8	1.9	5.3
Mining & Quarrying		0.0	0.0		0.0	0.0		0.0	0.0
Others			0.4			0.6			0.1
III. Activity not adequately described		1.9	1.0		2.1	1.2		1.4	0.6
Total	100	100	100	100	100	100	100	100	100

Source: Population Census, 1971, 1981 and 1991, CBS.

Agriculture is becoming progressively feminized. Many women engaged in family farms are still reported as economically not active. Nonetheless, even according to census figures, the proportion of female labor force in agriculture has increased between 1971 and 1991. In 1971, women constituted 30.4 percent of the agricultural labor force. That increased to 36.4 percent in 1981 and to 45 percent in 1991 (Table 4.8). Although female employment is increasing in the non-agricultural sector, comparatively a larger proportion of agricultural labor force are women.

Table 4.8 Sex Composition of Economically Active Population
by Industry

(In percent)

Industry	Male			Female		
	1971	1981	1991	1971	1981	1991
I. Agriculture & Forestry	69.6	63.6	55.0	30.4	36.4	45.0
II. Non Agriculture	90.5	85.7	79.8	9.5	14.3	20.2
Mining & Quarrying	86.1	73.3	79.4	13.9	26.7	20.6
Manufacturing	87.5	85.1	77.1	12.5	14.9	22.9
Elect. Gas & Water	98.4	95.2	93.6	1.6	4.9	6.4
Construction	97.2	94.1	89.1	2.8	5.9	10.9
Commerce	87.7	85.0	76.3	12.4	15.0	23.7
Transport & Communication	96.7	95.4	96.1	3.3	4.6	3.9
Finance	na	89.8	86.6	na	10.2	13.4
Personal & Community Services	96.1	85.5	79.0	3.9	14.5	21.0
Others	na	na	93.3	na	na	6.7
III. Not Stated	na	na	76.8	na	na	23.2
Total	70.8	65.4	59.6	29.2	34.6	40.4

Source: Population Census, 1971, 1981 and 1991, CBS.

Occupationally, more than 81 percent of the economically active population was engaged in farming and related occupations in 1991. That percentage was 74.7 for males and 90.5 for females in 1991, figures that are comparatively lower than corresponding ones observed in 1971 and 1981. The reduction of the economically active population in farming is compensated largely by increases in proportion service and sales workers and general laborers included in the category of production workers. The 1991 census indicates a nearly 10 percentage points decrease in farm and fishery workers compared to 1981. Professional and technical workers constitute a very small share of the total labor force (Table 4.9). Among non-agricultural female workers, the majority were engaged in the service sector. The proportion of females among the technical workers is still low (Table 4.10), while among the administrative workers it is lower.

Fig. 4.2 Sex Composition of Economically Active Population by Industry

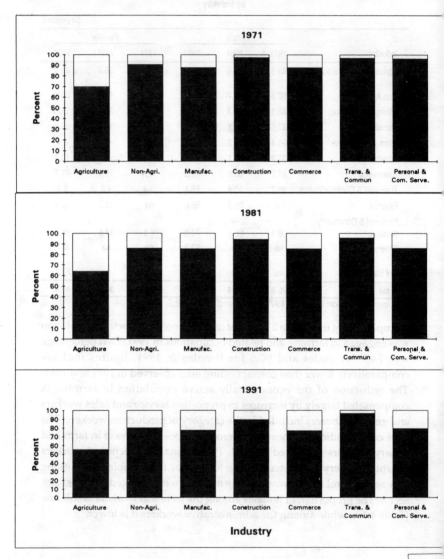

60

Table 4.9 Distribution of Economically Active Population by Broad Occupational Groups

(In percent)

Occupation	Total			Male			Female		
	1971	1981	1991	1971	1981	1991	1971	1981	1991
Farm/Fish workers	94.4	91.4	81.1	92.8	88.9	74.7	98.2	96.1	90.5
Professional/Technical workers	0.5	0.9	1.8	0.7	1.2	2.5	0.1	0.5	0.7
Administrative workersa/	0.0	0.1	0.3	0.0	0.1	0.5	--	0.0	0.1
Clerical workers	1.0	0.7	1.1	1.3	1.0	1.6	0.1	0.1	0.3
Sales workers	1.2	1.3	3.0	1.5	1.6	3.9	0.5	0.5	1.7
Service workers	0.7	0.2	6.2	0.8	0.3	7.8	0.4	0.1	3.8
Prod. workers/Labor	2.2	3.1	4.2	2.8	3.9	5.8	0.7	1.7	2.0
Unknown	--	1.7	0.3	--	3.0	0.3	--	1.0	0.3
Others			2.1			3.0			0.8
Total	**100.0**	**100.0**	**100.0**	**100.0**	**100.0**	**100.0**	**100.00**	**100.0**	**100.0**

Source: Population Census, 1971, 1981 and 1991, CBS.

a/ The figures are 0.02 for total and 0.03 for males in 1971, and 0.02 for females in 1981. As such not reflected in one digit.

Table 4.10 Sex Composition of Broad Occupational Groups

(In row percent)

Occupation	Male			Female		
	1971	1981	1991	1971	1981	1991
Farm/Fish workers	69.6	63.6	55.0	30.4	36.4	45.1
Professional/Technical	—	83.4	84.9	—	16.6	15.1
Administrative	95.8	93.4	90.7	4.2	6.6	9.3
Clerical workers	96.1	94.2	90.0	3.9	5.8	10.0
Sales workers	88.0	85.4	77.4	12.1	14.6	22.6
Service workers	84.3	85.5	74.9	15.7	14.5	25.1
Prod. workers/Labor	—	80.8	81.2	--	19.2	18.8
Unknown	—	84.9	64.1	--	15.1	35.9
Others		84.2			15.8
Total	**70.8**	**65.4**	**59.6**	**29.2**	**34.6**	**40.4**

Source: Population Census, 1971, 1981 and 1991, CBS.

Fig. 4.3 Sex Composition of Broad Occupational Groups

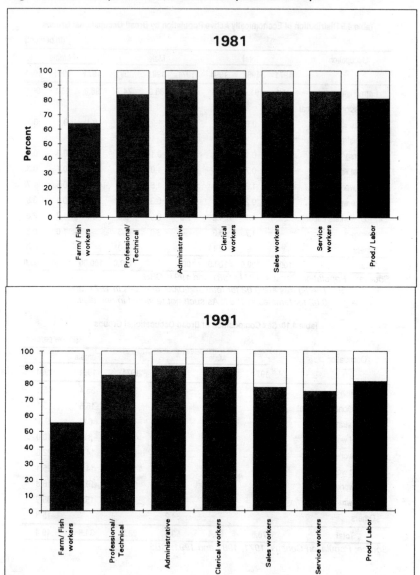

4.3 The Employment Status

The overwhelming majority of workers are still self-employed or own account workers while less than one percent are employers. The percentage of self-employed workers, which remained more or less constant at about 86 percent between 1971 and 1981, has decreased to 75 percent in 1991 (Table 4.11). That decrease is mainly accounted for by males. In other words, a larger proportion of women are self-employed than men.

There is a slow but perceptible change taking place in the employment status of the population. The proportions of both male and female employees in the population are increasing while that of the self-employed or unpaid family workers are decreasing (Table 4.11). This may signify a positive or negative trend, depending on whether those who move out of the self-employment are getting better jobs or just moving out because of impoverishment caused by flooding of the market by factory produced goods. Many traditional craft workers for example, have been ruined by the flood of plastic goods in the market.

Table 4.11 Employment Status of Economically Active Population

(In percent)

Status	Male			Female			Both		
	1971	1981	1991	1971	1981	1991	1971	1981	1991
Employer	0.6	0.9	0.7	0.2	0.4	0.4	0.5	0.7	0.6
Employee	11.7	11.8	27.8	3.6	3.8	12.0	9.3	9.1	21.4
Self-Employed	84.6	83.2	69.5	89.0	90.0	83.7	85.9	85.5	75.3
Family Worker	3.1	1.7	1.5	7.2	4.0	3.5	4.3	2.5	2.3
Not Stated	-	2.4	0.4	-	1.8	0.5	-	2.2	0.4
Total	100	100	100	100	100	100	100	100	100

Source: Population Census, 1971, 1981 and 1991, CBS.

Most male and female unpaid family workers are below 20 years of age. The proportion of men and women working as unpaid family workers decreases with increase in age. In the higher age groups the percentage of the male unpaid family worker is negligible. Furthermore, with an increase in age the percentage of male employers expands. That is also true of female employers although the increase in less significant (Table 4.12). It should, however, be noted that most women reported as self-employed are actually working as unpaid family workers. Women working in household farms

(In percent)

Table 4.12 Age Specific Employment Status

Male Age-Group	Employer			Employee			Self Employed			Unpaid Family Worker			Not Stated	
	1971	1981	1991	1971	1981	1991	1971	1981	1991	1971	1981	1991	1981	1991
10 - 14	0.5	0.2	0.3	7.2	4.4	24.7	83.3	90.7	64.3	9.1	3.5	10.2	1.3	0.6
15 - 19	0.2	0.4	0.3	10.7	9.3	26.7	83.1	84.4	68.6	6.1	3.7	3.8	2.3	0.5
20 - 24	0.5	0.6	0.5	14.9	14.2	30.8	80.6	79.4	66.6	4.1	2.8	1.7	3.0	0.5
25 - 29	0.5	0.8	0.6	15.2	16.9	34.3	81.8	77.5	63.7	2.5	1.8	0.9	3.0	0.5
30 - 34	0.5	0.9	0.7	13.4	16.2	33.3	84.5	79.0	65.1	1.6	1.2	0.6	2.8	0.4
35 - 39	0.5	1.0	0.8	12.8	15.0	31.7	85.6	80.6	66.7	1.1	0.7	0.4	2.6	0.4
40 - 44	0.7	1.1	0.8	11.6	13.0	28.1	87.0	83.0	70.4	0.7	0.5	0.4	2.4	0.4
45 - 49	0.8	1.2	0.9	11.3	11.9	24.5	87.5	84.2	74.0	0.4	0.4	0.3	2.2	0.3
50 - 54	0.5	1.2	0.8	9.4	10.4	20.0	81.6	85.9	78.5	0.5	0.4	0.4	2.1	0.3
55 - 59	-	1.4	1.1	-	9.3	17.2	-	86.8	80.9	-	0.4	0.6	2.0	0.3
60 - 64	1.1	1.5	1.2	8.9	8.6	15.4	88.9	87.5	82.2	1.1	0.4	0.9	2.0	0.3
65 +	1.4	1.8	1.9	7.1	6.2	13.6	91.4	89.6	82.7	-	0.5	1.4	1.8	0.4
Total	**0.6**	**0.9**	**0.7**	**11.7**	**11.8**	**27.8**	**84.6**	**83.2**	**69.5**	**3.1**	**1.7**	**1.5**	**2.4**	**0.4**

Contd...

64

Table 4.12 Age Specific Employment Status

(In percent)

Female Age-Group	Employer			Employee			Self Employed			Unpaid Family Worker			Not Stated[a]	
	1971	1981	1991	1971	1981	1991	1971	1981	1991	1971	1981	1991	1981	1991
10 - 14	-	0.2	0.2	2.5	2.1	10.5	84.9	90.9	76.7	12.6	5.4	12.0	1.4	0.6
15 - 19	0.4	0.2	0.2	3.0	3.5	11.5	87.5	88.5	83.1	9.1	5.9	4.7	1.9	0.5
20 - 24	0.5	0.3	0.3	3.5	4.5	12.7	88.9	88.9	84.0	7.1	4.3	2.6	2.0	0.4
25 - 29	0.6	0.3	0.3	4.0	4.9	13.6	89.7	88.9	83.6	5.8	3.7	2.1	2.1	0.4
30 - 34	-	0.4	0.4	4.2	5.0	13.7	90.9	89.2	83.7	5.0	3.3	1.9	2.1	0.4
35 - 39	-	0.4	0.4	4.1	4.8	13.1	90.9	89.8	84.4	5.0	3.1	1.7	2.0	0.4
40 - 44	-	0.5	0.4	5.0	4.3	11.9	90.1	90.3	85.6	5.0	3.0	1.8	1.9	0.4
45 - 49	-	0.5	0.5	4.3	4.2	10.7	91.4	90.6	86.6	4.3	2.9	1.9	1.8	0.4
50 - 54	-	0.6	0.5	3.3	3.7	9.6	91.7	91.2	87.6	5.0	2.8	2.0	1.7	0.4
55 - 59	-	0.6	0.6	-	4.4	9.1	-	91.6	87.6	-	2.7	2.2	1.7	0.4
60 - 64	-	0.8	0.9	3.6	3.1	8.8	92.9	92.4	87.2	3.6	2.2	2.6	1.5	0.5
65 +	-	0.8	1.5	5.3	2.1	8.6	89.5	94.1	86.3	5.3	1.7	3.1	1.4	0.6
Total	0.2	0.4	0.4	3.7	3.8	12.0	88.9	90.0	83.7	7.2	4.0	3.5	1.8	0.5

Source: Population Census, 1971, 1981 and 1991, CBS.
a) In 1971 there was no category of unstated.

65

or other household enterprises would not be perceived as unpaid family workers and reported so.

4.4 Socio-Economic Characteristics of the Working Population

An overwhelming majority of the workforce are married, illiterate and are between 24 and 64 years of age. A larger proportion of male workforce are literate (Table 4.13). Illeterate workforce is concentrated in agriculture. Modern sectors such as electricity, gas & water commerce, services & manufacturing have higher proportion of literate workforce.

It is evident that relatively small proportion of women workers are literate in all fields. Most men and women in various occupations are married. The proportion of married women are relatively lower in manufacturing. By age group, 10-24 year old female workers are getting concentrated in manufacturing. This confirms to the trends in other countries where the manufacturing sector tends to employ unmarried young women. A larger proportion of female children than male children are recruited to the workfore early.

Table 4.13 Socio-Economic Characteristics of the Economically Active Population by Industry (10 years and above)

Industry	Literacy		Ever married		10-14		15-24		25-64		65+	
	Male	Female	Male	Female	Male	Female	Male	Female	Male	Female	Male	Female
Agr. Forestry & Fish.	38.5	13.5	81.5	78.9	5.6	10.8	23.0	30.8	67.9	57.0	3.4	1.4
Mining & Quarrying	54.1	22.0	86.3	84.0	1.0	4.3	24.5	29.8	72.5	64.7	2.0	1.2
Manufacturing	52.8	27.0	79.6	62.4	3.8	11.0	27.9	44.6	66.1	43.5	2.1	0.9
Elec.,Gas & Water	88.1	83.1	86.8	79.8	0.2	0.8	16.9	29.5	82.3	69.5	0.6	0.3
Construction	49.1	15.8	85.0	79.3	1.9	8.2	22.4	30.7	74.1	60.3	1.6	0.8
Commerce	74.0	36.1	84.3	89.0	1.6	2.5	20.8	22.5	74.8	73.3	2.8	1.7
Transport & Comm.	73.3	60.0	85.4	77.6	0.7	4.7	23.3	30.5	75.5	64.1	0.6	0.8
Finance & Bussiness Service	94.6	93.6	88.3	86.5	0.2	0.5	11.0	14.8	88.3	84.3	0.5	0.3
Personal & Comm. Service	61.3	30.1	80.8	76.6	4.0	9.6	23.9	30.4	70.7	59.0	1.3	1.0
Others	60.8	48.0	75.4	79.8	2.6	3.6	31.7	31.7	64.6	63.6	1.1	1.1
Industry not stated	58.6	26.4	77.3	73.0	5.0	13.2	26.1	30.2	66.9	54.6	2.0	2.1
Total	44.8	15.2	81.5	78.7	5.0	10.6	23.2	30.7	68.8	57.3	3.0	1.4

Source: Population Census, 1991.

V. WOMEN INDUSTRIAL WORKERS

Nepal is at an early stage of industrial development. According to recorded statistics, manufacturing contributes to about 15 percent of the industrial output and to about six percent of the GDP. As per the 1991 census, the manufacturing sector accounted for less than three percent of male and only 1.2 percent of female employment (Table 4.7). Those figures, however, underestimate the contribution of cottage and household industries towards both GDP and employment. The Nepal Rastra Bank Multi-purpose Household Budget Survey (1989, p. 58) reported about 4.3 percent of the male and 2.9 percent of the female workers in the manufacturing sector. Occupationally, even urban women are mainly employed in agriculture. According to that survey, the next largest group of women workers was composed of those in the sales and services sector. The third largest group was constituted by women wage laborers working in the areas of construction, transportation and communications.

5.1 The Informal Sector

A significant proportion of manufacturing in Nepal takes place within the household. There are numerous small, unregistered production entities engaged in the production of a variety of products both for home consumption as well as for local sales. Also, the production of a few selected export products such as carpets is widely diffused. Their operations are generally restricted to off-farm hours and hence employment is only part-time. Units are widely scattered, but predominantly located in the Hills and Mountains, along with major clusters in urban areas (UNIDO, 1988).

The separation between "typically" male or female industries in the informal sector was not very clear in 1987. Indeed, as per a number of case studies conducted by UNIDO in 1987, establishment size of such units in the informal sector varied considerably — from that employing a single person to 10 persons. On the whole, female employment dominated slightly in the industries visited at the level of 51.6 percent. In the case of handloom weaving establishments, women clearly dominated in the work force, though some of such units employed more men than women. Female employment in mineral and agro-based industries, varied according to the location of the industry and size of the units. Tarai units usually employed significantly less women. While family labor played an important role in all household based units, most of them also employed wage-labor. Productivity in most of the household industries was very low (Islam/ Shrestha, 1986). Very few women could earn more than Rs. 2,000 per month from such activities, even from full-time employment (UNIDO, 1988).

5.2 *Employment in the Formal Sector*

The growth of the manufacturing sector in Nepal has been slow and arduous. The industrial structure did, however, mark a substantial change in the eighties. A decline in the share of the food and allied sub-sector has been noted as also rapid gains in textile and garment, plastics and electric goods supply sub-sectors. Despite the low level of skills and cultural inhibitions, an increasing number of women are joining the ranks of industrial workers. In 1976/77, women had constituted 11.2 percent of the total labor force in manufacturing industries. That proportion went up to 17 percent in 1986/89 and to 23.0 percent in 1990/91. The number of female workers has increased more than six-fold — i.e, from 5,557 in 1976/77 to 36,729 in 1990/91. The number of male workers during the same time span increased less than threefold (Table 5.1).

Female employment is not increasing uniformly in all sectors. Textile and garment industries have been one of the fastest growing in the country with an increasing number of women being absorbed by them. The share of female workers according to these statistics however, is increasing only slowly, from about 36 percent in 1976/77 to 40 percent in 1990/91. The proportion of female workers in 1990/91 in the plastics, chemicals and pharmaceutical industries, as also in the field of metallic products, declined as compared to 1976/77. In food and allied industries the number of female workers has remained virtually constant. Women's employment in the formal manufacturing sector is, however, increasing in all other product groups.

In 1987, women's employment in industries in the organized sector depended less on type of industry than on its location, size of investment and degree of mechanization (Rana and Shah, 1987). Thus, Rana and Shah note that while the Bansbari Leather and Shoe Factory of Kathmandu had 15.6 percent female employees, the Universal Leather Pvt. Ltd of Biratnagar had only 7.0 percent. Similarly, the Gosali Kapada (Textile) Udyog of Pokhara, with little mechanization, had 89 percent of female workers compared to about 26 percent in the Balaju Kapada Udyog with power looms in Kathmandu and zero percent in the more mechanized and automated Ashoka Textile of Biratnagar. With mechanization women workers seem to be immediately replaced by male workers.

Table 5.1 Structure of Female Employment - Manufacturing Survey
(1976/77,1986/87 and 1990/91)

(In Numbers)

Industry	1976/77			1986/87			1990/91		
	Total	Female	Female % of Total	Total	Female	Female % of Total	Total	Female	Female % of Total
Food and Allied Drinks and	20021	2249	11.3	18454	1959	10.6	17789	2257	12.7
Tobacco	5158	106	2.1	8446	1137	13.5	6945	554	8.0
Textile and Wearing apparel	3457	1248	36.1	35639	11881	33.3	55649	22084	39.7
Wood, Paper and Printing	5793	318	5.5	11829	690	5.8	7799	36	5.6
Plastics, Chemicals & Pharmaceuticals	441	76	17.2	7361	946	12.9	7445	1069	14.4
Non-metallic mineral Products	6019	860	14.3	45757	6573	14.4	58792	10130	17.2
Metallic Products	1389	89	6.4	5540	105	1.9	3259	106	3.3
Electrical Machinery and Supplies	n.a	n.a	n.a	838	57	6.8	843	24	2.8
Activities n.e.c	7341	611	8.3	888	68	7.7	1089	69	6.3
GRAND TOTAL	49619	5557	11.2	134758	23416	17.4	159610	36729	23.0

Source: Survey of Manufacturing Industries, CBS, 1976/77, 1986/87, 1990/91.
Note: n.e.c = not elsewhere classified.

The pattern of female employment also seemed to be governed by the size of industrial investment (Table 5.2). Female employment was concentrated in those industries where the fixed capital investment was the lowest. That meant that the majority of female workers received low pay.

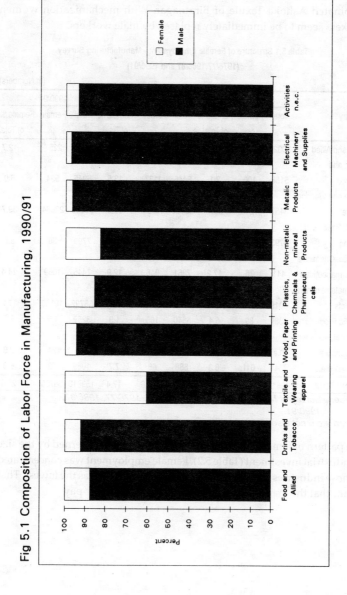

Fig 5.1 Composition of Labor Force in Manufacturing, 1990/91

Weaving is a major activity for women.

Table 5.2 Size of Establishment by Investment and Employment, 1981/82

Fixed capital investment (in million Rs.)	No. of establishment	Percent	No. of employees			
			Male		Female	
			Total	Percent	Total	Percent
0.0 - 0.5	4,628	94.2	42,069	59.0	6,193	63.8
0.6 - 0.8	96	2.0	4,166	5.8	452	4.7
0.9 - 2.0	95	1.9	5,430	7.6	985	10.1
2.1 - 10.0	69	1.2	10,708	15.0	1,299	13.4
10 and over	24	0.5	8,969	12.6	779	8.1
Total	4,908	-	71,342	88.0	9,708	12.0

Source: HMG/ADB, Nepal Industrial Sector Study, 1985.

The majority of women in the formal sector worked as semi-skilled and unskilled workers (Shrestha Neeru 1983). In virtually all food, drink, tobacco and match industries female workers were mainly concentrated in packing the finished product and in related processes. The large scale textile factories are no exception. For example, at the Hetauda textile factory, with 50 percent women in the work force, there were very few women performing supervisory functions and none at all at the managerial level (Shrestha M. 1990).

The concentration of women in low-paid, unskilled jobs may be attributed to low literacy, low skill levels and also to social bias regarding the appropriateness of employing female workers for certain jobs but not others. A survey of 5.0 percent of existing industries conducted by UNIDO in 1987 concluded that employers were biased against female employees. Among the reasons provided for women being under-represented in industry were: low literacy; reluctance of families to send females into factory work; legal restriction on female employment after 6 P.M.; the unwillingness of educated females to migrate/travel to work, or engage in dirty jobs; lower work efficiency of the female worker as compared to her male counterpart; a high rate of absenteeism due to maternity or domestic reasons; and the loss of skill development represented by women who leave their jobs upon marriage. The reasons that were advanced concerning the concentration of women workers in certain jobs were: female temperament, docility, nimble hands suitable for jobs such as carpet weaving, nursing, sewing by hand, weaving, knitting, packaging, tea-leaf picking, etc.

While a number of the reasons advanced above can be substantiated (e.g. their lower educational levels), others (e.g. their alleged lower efficiency level) are reflections of gender bias. Those responses also indicate the pattern of social bias of employers in choice of employees for various forms of work. The government, for its part, tends to reinforce such biases by providing training to women only in such skills as considered to be clearly women-specific. For example, Table 5.3, which provides statistics on Cottage and Village Industries Development Board trainees between 1985/86 - 1989/90, clearly indicates the concentration of female trainees in textile and basket-weaving related skills.

Table 5.3 Women's Participation in Cottage & Village Industries
Dev. Board Skill Development Trainings (Year s1985/86-1989/90)

Programmes	Number of Trainees	Average % of Female Trainees
Weaving	2266	70
Readymade garments	745	30
Wool Carpets & Spinning	576	70
Knitwear & Hosiery	865	80
Dyeing & Printing	53	5 - 20
Other Textile	60	50 - 60
Basketry	266	50 - 60
Blacksmithy & Metal Handicrafts	187	0 - 10
Food storage & Preservation	103	20 - 40
Ceramics	42	20
Handmade paper	39	20
Pottery	8	20
Bee-keeping, honey processing	51	10
Electronics & Mechanicals	28	0
Carpentry	66	0
Refresher, On the job, new design and others	1902	0 - 20
Total	**7213**	

Source: Progress Report, CIDB, 1990.

Working Conditions

Only scattered information is available on the working conditions in these industrial establishments. A survey (Basnet, 1991), of 66 women engaged in nine industrial establishments located in the Kathmandu Valley has the following data on working conditions and on the work place. About 55

percent of women workers had permanent jobs, about 17 percent were
temporary employees and 29 percent were casual laborers. Only 20 percent
had been promoted to higher levels. About 29 percent believed that they
were getting as much pay as male employees. They worked under difficult
physical conditions and more than one-third of those interviewed said they
had experienced some work-related health problems. Only about 33 percent
of them received some facilities additional to wages (Table 5.4). Only about
14 percent were trade union members while 17 percent were aware about
trade unions. Other studies on working conditions depict no better situation
(eg. Ojha, 1984, Joshi, 1985, Thacker, 1992).

Table 5.4 Some Indicators on Work Status of the Female Industrial Workers

Particulars	Number	Percent
Nature of Jobs		
Permanent	36	54.5
Temporary	11	16.7
Daily wages	19	28.8
Promotions		
Promoted	13	19.7
Not promoted	56	80.3
Pay Status		
Equal Pay	19	28.8
Not Equal	47	71.2
Kind of Wage		
Daily	26	39.4
Monthly	40	60.6
Satisfaction		
Yes	55	83.8
No	11	16.7
Health Status		
Sick	23	34.8
Not sick	43	65.2
Facilities		
Additional facilities	22	33.3
No facilities	24	36.4
No response	20	31.4

Source: Basnet, April, 1991.

Wool spinning - An early start.

Social Characteristics of the Female Industrial Workers:

As per the above survey (Basnet, 1991) almost 71 percent of women employees in these industries worked because of poverty. Almost 29 percent had no other bread winners in their household (Table 5.5).

Table 5.5 Reasons for Working

Causes	Number	Percent
No other earners in the household	19	28.80
For supplementary income	41	62.12
Other causes	5	7.57
No response	1	1.51
Total	**66**	**100.00**

Source: Basnet, 1991.

About 52 percent of women engaged in such industries were illiterate, about 15 percent had completed school and about 11 percent had college education. Eighty percent had learnt their trade informally through work and only 20 percent had received some form of formal training. About 55 percent were married, 29 percent were unmarried, 9 percent were widowed and 6 percent were single.

More than 60 percent were between 20 and 34 years of age. About 12 percent were child laborers (Table 5.6).

Table 5.6 Age Distribution of Female Workers

Age	Number	Percent
10 - 14	8	12.12
15 - 19	8	12.12
20 - 24	13	19.69
25 - 29	16	24.24
30 - 34	11	16.66
35 - 39	6	9.09
40 - 44	-	-
45 +	4	6.09
Total	**66**	**100.00**

Source: Basnet, 1991.

Wage Rates in Urban Areas

Not enough statistics are available on wage rates in general. Nepal Rastra Bank does collect some wage statistics from indivisual urban areas such as Kathmandu, Biratnagar, Bhairahawa, Nepalgunj etc. (See Annex B).

Although these figures tend to under estimate the market wage rates because they are collected from large construction sites and labor contractors, they are presented here with the conviction that they at least represent the trend. Industrial wages that are reported are usually close to the government fixed minimum, without gender breakdowns Table 5.7 below features trends in real wages in four towns of Nepal, from different parts of the country. According to these figures, real wages in the manufacturing sector have actually declined in the period 1991/92-1992/93 due to rapid inflation rates. Between 1987/88 and 1990/91, they had risen substantially. Where descrimination exists in the industrial sector, it is in the nature of employment. While most men are employed as permanent workers and as skilled laborers, most women are employed at piece rates and thus debarred from regular salary and other benefits.

Table 5.7. Real Wage Rates of unskilled labor in the Industrial Sector (At 1987/88 prices) a/
(Monthly)

(In NRs.)

Fiscal Year	Kathamandu	Biratnagar	Bairahawa	Nepalgunj
1980/81	398.2	530.6	408.2	492.7
1981/82	411.9	478.6	408.5	493.5
1982/83	416.2	416.2	416.2	499.2
1983/84	395.3	392.8	392.8	475.7
1984/85	474.4	453.8	442.8	465.6
1985/86	406.3	409.4	409.4	409.4
1986/87	354.3	401.3	476.0	364.0
1987/88	425.0	425.0	450.0	402.5
1988/89	490.6	497.2	470.6	472.9
1989/90	424.0	458.6	458.6	458.6
1990/91	579.8	629.9	629.9	629.9
1991/92	479.9	516.1	516.1	516.1
1992/93	522.6	583.3	580.4	535.7

Source : a/ Calculated on the basis of Annex B and CPI based deflator for respective areas and years from Nepal Rastra Bank Quarterly Bulletins for various years.

Carpet weaving - Generates additional income.

The agricultural and construction wage labor market does show a clear gender discrimination. For example, inspite of the increasing work opportunities in carpets and garments for women in the Kathmandu valley, the male/female wage differentials have increased in the agricultural and construction sectors except in 1987/88 - 1989/90 period, when there was a rapid rise in wages in general (Table 5.8). Biratnagar, in the east and Nepalgunj in the western Tarai also show similar trends. Only in Bhairahawa the male/female wage differentials have declined in last three years. It seems that in general male/female wage differentials increase when generally wage rates fall, signifying a fall in the demand for labor.

Table 5.8 : Female Wage Rates as Proportion of Male Wage Rates

(in percent)

Year	Agriculture				Construction			
	Kath-mandu	Birat-nagar	Bhair-ahawa	Nepal-gunj	Kath-mandu	Birat-nagar	Bhair-ahawa	Nepal-gunj
1980/81	66.6	90.2	100.0	88.6	-	-	-	-
1981/82	67.5	91.4	100.0	88.1	-	-	-	-
1982/83	74.4	91.7	86.9	86.8	-	- ,	-	-
1983/84	75.0	93.0	84.1	83.5	-	-	-	-
1984/85	81.9	89.0	88.0	81.2	-	-	-	-
1985/86	79.9	96.3	81.0	88.3	-	-	-	-
1986/87	79.9	100.0	81.3	93.7	-	100.0	-	-
1987/88	100.0	93.3	89.4	100.0	100.0	-	89.4	-
1988/89	100.0	88.0	85.6	83.7	92.4	88.0	85.0	-
1989/90	94.1	96.2	91.5	92.5	95.2	91.1	85.5	-
1990/91	77.5	89.1	100.0	86.8	85.5	89.9	92.2	93.6
1991/92	75.0	86.8	100.0	83.3	87.7	88.3	100.0	91.1
1992/93	63.2	88.1	100.0	83.2	89.3	89.4	100.0	88.1

Source: Table 5.9.

A 35 percent fall (Table 5.9) in female real agricultural wage rate between 1989/90-1992/93 in the Kathmandu valley calls for some explanation. One reason may be fall in the demand in agricultural labor in general in the valley due to the shortage of agricultural land. Inflow of male labor from the neighboring areas and foreign labor may also have depressed the female wage rates. Employment of girls at lower wages, as adult women move to industrial employment, may be a third cause of this labor market depression. All of the above however, are possibilities which could be rejected or accepted only after a field study.

Table 5.9. Real Wage Rates in the Agriculture and Construction Sector(At 1987/88 prices)

(Daily)

(In NRs.)

Fiscal Year	Hills				Tarai											
	Kathmandu				Birathagar				Bhairahawa				Nepalgunj			
	Agriculture		Construction		Agriculture		Construction		Agriculture		Construction		Agriculture		Construction.	
	Male	Female	Male	Female	Male	Female	Male	Female	Male	Female	Male	Female	Male	Female	Male	Female
1980/81	29.9	19.9	-	-	20.4	18.4	-	-	16.3	16.3	-	-	18.4	16.3	-	-
1981/82	27.4	18.5	-	-	22.1	20.2	-	-	16.2	16.2	-	-	21.8	19.2	-	-
1982/83	31.2	23.2	-	-	19.2	17.6	-	-	16.0	13.9	-	-	21.2	18.4	-	-
1983/84	30.4	22.8	-	-	22.7	21.1	-	-	18.9	15.9	-	-	22.4	18.7	-	-
1984/85	32.1	26.3	-	-	26.3	23.4	-	-	18.3	16.1	-	-	23.4	19.0	-	-
1985/86	31.3	25.0	-	-	24.4	23.5	-	-	18.4	14.9	-	-	21.4	18.9	-	-
1986/87	27.3	21.8	32.5	-	22.4	22.4	22.4	22.4	21.4	17.4	-	-	19.0	17.8	-	-
1987/88	35.0	35.0	35.0	35.0	22.5	21.0	-	-	23.5	21.0	23.5	21.0	21.0	21.0	-	-
1988/89	37.0	37.0	36.9	34.1	23.4	20.6	23.4	20.6	25.7	22.0	18.7	15.9	25.7	21.5	-	-
1989/90	34.0	32.0	33.5	31.9	23.7	22.8	23.7	21.6	25.9	23.7	17.2	14.7	28.0	25.9	28.0	-
1990/91	40.0	31.0	39.9	34.1	25.6	22.8	27.6	24.8	25.6	25.6	25.6	23.6	29.5	25.6	29.5	27.6
1991/92	36.0	27.0	35.9	31.5	24.2	21.0	27.4	24.2	24.2	24.2	24.2	24.2	25.2	21.0	24.8	22.6
1992/93	38.0	24.0	37.5	33.5	25.3	22.3	28.3	25.3	23.8	23.8	23.8	23.8	23.2	19.3	25.3	22.3

Source: Calculated on the basis of Annex B and CPI based deflator for respective areas and years from Nepal Rastra Bank Quarterly Bulletins for various years.

- denotes not available

Fig. 5.2 Real Wage Rates (At 1987/88 Prices)

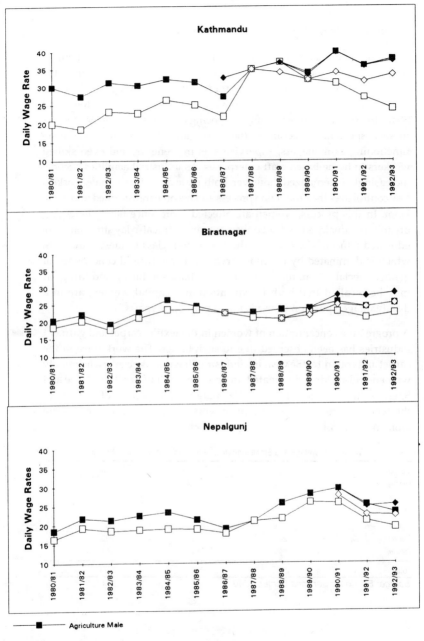

Industrial Transformation and Women

Home-based industries are either progressively dying due to competition from imported products or being replaced by organized formal units. On the one hand, the displacement of traditional crafts by light industry is causing the replacement of female workers by male laborers (Rana and Shah, 1989). On the other, women are being converted into wage laborers in such specialized sectors as the carpet industry. Women have been functioning as managers, supervisors, entrepreneurs, and even skilled workers in home-based craft enterprises. As industrial activities become increasingly externalized, however, both male as well as female workers lose control over the production process and become transformed into wage labor. In this process, women are affected more since newly emerging organised industries need not only more capital but also lay stress on more educated and mobile laborers. The managerial class in these industries, which is dominated by the Indo-Aryan and westernised conceptions of gender specialisation, reinforce their own biases in hiring and firing. It may be recalled that both in education and capital women, are in a disadvantaged position vis-a-vis their male counterparts.

A progressive concentration of women in the textile, carpet and garment industries has been observed due to such biases. The work force in the carpet and cotton-textile weaving industries have become overwhelmingly women-and-children dominated. In units financed under the Cottage and Small Industry Project, for example, more than 65 percent of workers in the woolen sector and 59 percent of workers in the cotton sector were women (Table 5.10).

Table 5.10 Cottage and Small Industries, Phase I Employment by Sector

Sector	Male	Female	Total
Woolen	410	779	1189
Cotton	367	536	903
Metal	266	22	288
Agro	272	65	337
Forest	241	49	290
Others	599	165	764
Total	2155	1616	3771

Source: Economic Services Center, 1990.

According to a recent survey (Thacker, 1992) the carpet industry in the Kathmandu valley had 66 percent women workers, but nearly 97.8 percent of these women were piece rate while only 14 percent of men were so. These women were overwhelmingly young (below 22 years of age), illiterate and worked for reasons of poverty. Cheating by the employers on payments of salary and wages was rampant. Women benefitted little from mechanisation, as men progressively took the mechanised jobs.

Women working in such industries are not only married but often go to work with their younger children in tow. Such children either work with their mothers or play around the loom. The environmental conditions in such units are very unwholesome and ventilation in the work place is poor and hence harmful to their health. Wool spinning is performed at home in conditions that are not safe from a health point of view harming both the mother and her children.

Thus, an increasing number of women are entering the work force in the formal manufacturing sector because of economic need. However, they are mainly concentrated in low-skill, menial and repetitive jobs and in the lower echelons of the industrial hierarchy in what is virtually an extension of their household activities. Even in the carpet industry, where it is a highly skilled job, women are still treated as unskilled and intensely exploited by the factory owners. Additionally, as international competition in such industries is very keen, wages are kept down.

The patriarchal value and patrilineal inheritance systems pervades the psychology of policy makers - the majority of both men and women, either at the work place or at home (see CERID, 1986 a and b for a survey in attitude). Physical work outside the household is viewed as degrading to the family status. As such, women who work outside the home are looked down (Kemp, 1986). In effect, that extends their inferior status from the household to the work place. In other words, working women have to bear with inferior status in the factory, as well as with the double work-burden at home. Consequently, women generally opt for the non-working status unless there is an urgent need for an additional bread earner for the family or if there is no alternative source of household income. On the other hand, working outside their households enables a woman to have not only some control over the fruits of her own labor but also to create some social space for herself. The net outcome for individual women's status, as a consequence of her increased power within the household, on the one hand, and, the decreased public status of the household, on the other, in such a shift from home-based to market-base work is not clear. Discussions in other countries have tended to produce sound arguments both on the positive (for example see Lim, 1983) and on negative side (for example see Benerjee, 1991, Salaff, 1981 or Siegel 1983). In Nepal not much information is available on how these working women perceive their own status vis-a-vis non-working women, and how the community views such working women.

VI. DEVELOPMENT IMPACT AND INTER-DISTRICT VARIATIONS

In this chapter an attempt is made to analyze inter-district variations of selected demographic and socio-economic variables, as per census results. The chief purpose in doing so is to evaluate the impact of various development initiatives on demographic characteristics.

Nepal is currently implementing its Eighth Five Year Plan (1992/93-1996/97). In all her 75 administrative districts a number of development programs are underway. However, the number and type of programs vary from district to district. We assume that these development programs would have an impact on population behavior. In other words, the socio-economic characteristics of the population should register a change over time. The degree of change may naturally vary depending on whether or not there are such programs, the length of time they have been in effect and the scope and effect of their implementation.

Additionally, population behavior may be influenced by the impact of physical and social infra-structural facilities such as roads, schools, hospitals, etc., as well as their general exposure to the world beyond their village or district. As discussed in Chapter III and IV, urbanization does seem to have had a positive effect both on female literacy rates or on reduction of fertility. The original project objectives in the current endeavour included examining, on the basis of district-level data, whether specific interventions such as family planning and the establishment of schools by NGOs or the government was closely related to social and demographic characteristics in districts selected. Such a methodology had, however, to be largely abandoned since no data was available on the history of either NGO interventions or government programs. Indeed, most data on health and education services are mainly government-registered related. Considering only government-sector schools or health posts, the three districts of the Kathmandu Valley appear to have the largest number of school-going age children per school or population per health post. If one calculates the number of health posts per thousand population, for example in Bhaktapur district, it does not differ very much from a similar variable for more remote districts. This clearly seems implausible. That state of affairs is probably explained by the fact that private schools or clinics which proliferate in the districts of the Kathmandu Valley are not included in those statistics.

Nevertheless, even if one lacks data on the exact number of private health clinics and nursing homes, for example, the number of registered schools or health posts in the Kathmandu district are among the highest in the country. Therefore the absolute number of registered schools or health posts are chosen as indicators of health and education facilities for this district level analysis.

Table 6.1 Some Indicators of Infrastructural Development by District

District	Roads 1990 a/		Number of		Totall Population in '000 d/ (1991)
	Km.	Per 1000 sq.km.	Health Posts and Hospitals b/ (1991/92)	Schools c/ (1991)	
Mountain					
Rasuwa	.107	69	12	109	37
Manang	0	0	12	38	5
Bajhang	0	0	18	272	139
Solukhumbu	0	0	16	194	97
Dolpa0	0	12	95	25	
Hills					
Dhankuta	89	100	20	315	146
Ilam	161	94	16	361	229
Kavre	93	67	21	490	324
Dhading	122	63	24	476	278
Baglung	0	0	20	373	232
Gorkha	35	10	20	504	253
Surkhet	89	36	19	402	226
Pyuthan	95	73	17	281	175
Doti	0	0	20	260	167
Baitadi	19	12	18	300	201
Kathmandu	441	112	31	810	675
Lalitpur	169	44	18	468	253
Bhaktapur	119	100	20	232	133
Tarai					
Morang	310	167	30	516	675
Sarlahi	114	90	21	351	493
Rupandehi	226	166	22	351	522
Bardiya	108	53	15	238	290
Kanchanpur	207	129	15	193	258

Sources: a) Department of Roads (1991) Nepal Road Statistics 1990.
        b) Department of Health (1992) Health Information Bulletin.
        c) Educational Statistics 1991.
        d) Population Census, 1991.

For comparative purposes, we have selected 23 districts from among the country's total of 75; four each from the five development regions of the kingdom, plus the three districts of the Kathmandu Valley. Though such a selection is admittedly somewhat arbitrary, a proper geographical representation has been ensured. Two Hill and one each Mountain and Tarai districts have been included in the sample from each development region. Changes that have occurred in selected demographic and socio-economic characteristics over the decades are then compared across the districts.

It is assumed that the opening of schools and the provision of road and health services have produced some definite change in the socio-economic profile of the population. Such a system ignores the time dimension. In other words, it does not take into account the length of time that has lapsed since such roads have been built or the specific development interventions started in those districts. A district with a history of road access for 10 years may be expected to be more advanced in terms of education, knowledge about family planning, etc., than one where a road has been build only a year ago. However, given the dearth of reliable information, that was felt to be the most appropriate method for the current analysis. We are naturally conscious that such analysis is rather crude. Nonetheless, it is a beginning towards a cross-section analysis.

6.1 Sex Ratio

Sex ratio (males per 100 females), as already discussed, is a valuable indicator of social behavior towards women. Sex ratio of one hundred means that there are one hundred males for each one hundred females. A sex ratio that is considerably above or below one hundred thus indicates a distortion of the demographic sex balance. The sex balance of any given locale tends to change due to migration, apart, of course, from factors affecting birth and death rates. In-migration of males tend to increase the sex ratio in favor of males whereas out-migration tends to have the reverse effect. Development work at any particular venue usually attracts male labor from labor surplus areas and triggers changes in the sex ratio of the concerned area.

Table 6.2 Sex Ratio of Population by District, 1971-91

(Male per 100 Female)

District	Sex Ratio		
	1971	1981	1991
Mountain			
Rasuwa	102.42	108.24	106.90
Manang	110.53	101.87	108.35
Bajhang	101.74	100.65	92.01
Solukhumbu	99.69	102.15	97.24
Dolpa	99.17	108.46	103.19
Hills			
Dhankuta	97.36	104.06	97.00
Ilam	101.91	106.61	101.35
Kavre	99.18	103.50	97.11
Dhading	102.41	104.77	98.57
Baglung	95.23	99.68	87.27
Gorkha	99.05	98.23	92.48
Surkhet	99.45	100.69	98.17
Pyuthan	94.20	96.48	87.23
Doti	96.67	96.38	93.71
Baitadi	103.09	102.80	92.33
Kathmandu	108.28	117.31	108.42
Lalitpur	102.96	112.71	102.81
Bhaktapur	105.49	105.00	100.79
Tarai			
Morang	110.05	108.59	103.40
Sarlahi	103.49	106.86	107.20
Rupandehi	107.65	107.94	102.74
Bardiya	108.40	109.16	102.46
Kanchanpur	113.67	122.92	101.67

Sources: Population Censuses, 1971, 1981 and 1991.

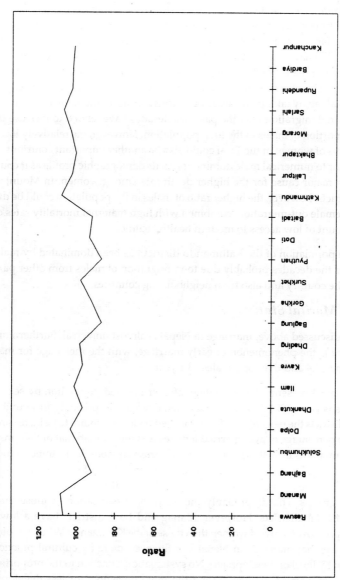

Fig 6.1 Sex Ratio of Population by District, 1991 (Male per 100 Female)

Sex ratios in most districts under consideration were found to be changing over time. In a number of districts it was unexplainably high in 1981 (Table 6.2). Tarai, some of the Mountain and Kathmandu Valley districts were found to have higher sex ratios than other Hill districts, irrespective of the length of roads per 1000 square km. and the number of schools or health posts. The observed differentials in the sex ratio among districts can be explained by taking into account various factors. In the Tarai, external and internal migration over the past two decades have tended to increase the proportion of males in the total population. However, the relatively lower status of women in the Tarai could also be another important contributing factor to numerical male domination in its demographic profile as it could be a major cause for the higher death rate among women. In Mountain districts, however, the higher ratio of males in the population could be due to female out-migration, combined with high maternal mortality rates on account of low access to modern health facilities.

The population of the Kathmandu district has been dominated by males over the decades probably due to in-migration of males from other parts of the country and also from neighbouring countries.

6.2 Marital Status

As discussed above, marriage in Nepal is almost universal. Furthermore, there is the phenomenon of early marriage, with the mean age for male being 21.4 and that for females 18.1 years.

Table 6.3 presents the percentage of ever married population by sex for census years 1971-1991 for the selected districts. Surprisingly, in a number of districts the percentage of ever married males was found to be increasing. The percentage of ever married females was higher than that of their male counterparts in all the districts and at all census periods. In the three districts of the Kathmandu Valley, however, the percentage of ever married was found to be marginally less than in most other districts in the land, across the groups. That is probably the result of urbanization in those three particular districts. However, Manag and Ilam districts have a lower proportion of married women than those of the Kathmandu Valley. It would appear that marriage in Nepal is influenced more by cultural practices than by level of development. No systematic distinction in the proportion of ever married women among the more developed or less developed districts was observed (Table 6.3).

Table 6.3 Ever-married Population by Sex and by District, 1971-91
(Population 10 years and above)

District	Male				Female		
	1971	1981	1991		1971	1981	1991
Mountain							
Rasuwa	56.4	62.8	64.8		63.6	73.5	73.7
Manang	47.1	59.2	64.1		53.8	63.5	61.0
Bajhang	62.8	73.0	67.7		75.0	83.0	78.8
Solukhumbu	50.9	54.8	57.9		59.2	64.0	64.3
Dolpa	55.1	63.0	62.5		63.6	69.0	69.6
Hills							
Dhankuta	51.4	58.5	58.6		60.7	67.3	64.9
Ilam	47.2	53.4	55.7		55.7	63.9	62.7
Kavre	57.8	62.5	63.3		68.0	73.8	71.2
Dhading	57.6	62.8	65.2		68.8	75.7	73.8
Baglung	53.0	62.6	62.0		66.4	73.5	71.1
Gorkha	56.4	64.6	61.3		67.9	74.9	70.7
Surkhet	54.4	67.6	63.0		64.6	78.8	71.4
Pyuthan	55.3	67.7	63.5		66.9	76.1	72.8
Doti	59.2	67.7	64.5		74.5	80.7	77.5
Baitadi	60.8	61.6	66.2		74.6	78.9	78.5
Kathmandu	53.6	58.4	54.9		63.1	70.1	65.3
Lalitpur	55.7	59.4	57.7		65.0	71.0	65.7
Bhaktapur	58.1	61.2	60.2		67.1	71.4	67.3
Tarai							
Morang	58.3	60.3	59.1		68.3	73.3	69.1
Sarlahi	63.3	72.1	68.3		76.4	85.4	81.8
Rupandehi	70.6	75.5	70.7		79.7	84.6	79.4
Bardiya	58.5	68.6	64.2		68.5	76.8	72.5
Kanchanpur	60.9	68.5	64.0		70.5	81.1	73.9

Sources: Population Census, 1991

Fig 6.2 Ever Married Female Population by District

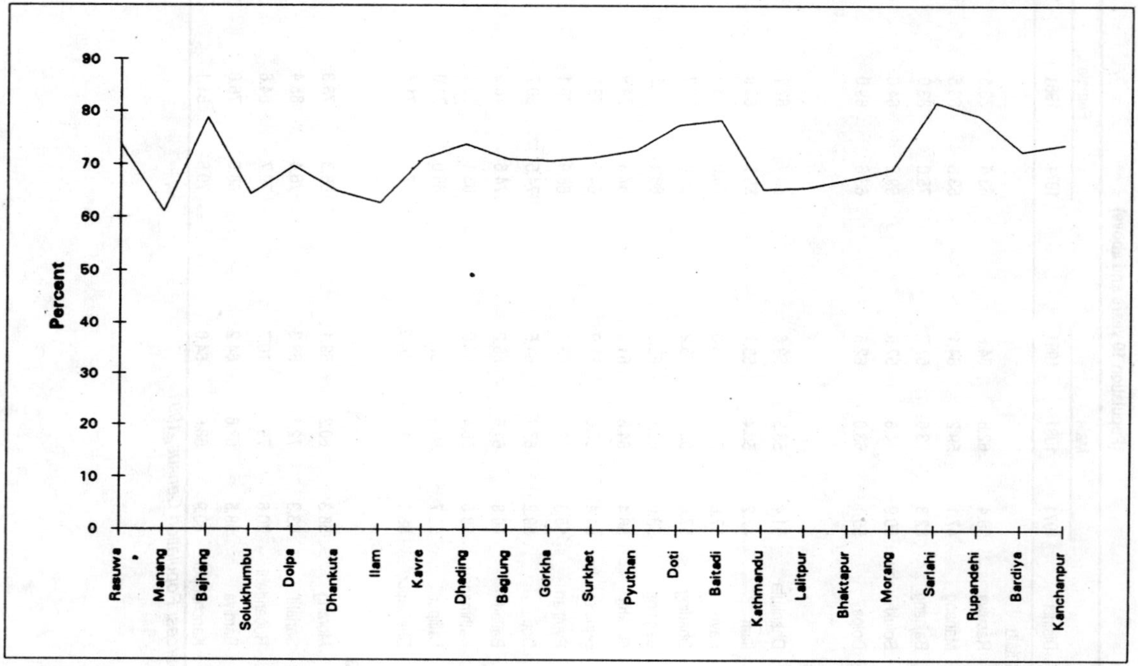

6.3 Fertility and Family Planning

The mean number of children born to ever married women between the ages of 15-49 was uniformly high for all the districts, indicating no positive relationship between stage of development and fertility reduction (Table 6.4). Neither did there seem to be any correlation between knowledge about family planning devices and fertility rate. Thus, Dolpa, Kathmandu, Baglung, Gorkha and Baitadi districts were all at the lower reaches of the fertility scale despite their widely differing level of development. Child survival rates were found to be significantly higher than the rest only in the Ilam and Kathmandu districts. The relatively low child survival rate in the Sarlahi district is surprising.

6.4 Literacy Status

The literacy rate of the population 6 years of age and above is presented in Table 6.5. From that table it may be observed that the literacy rate is increasing over time in all the districts and for both sexes. However, male literacy rates are considerably higher than female literacy rates in all districts at all census periods.

Naturally, the districts of the Kathmandu Valley have much higher literacy rates as compared to the other districts. That is true for both sexes. It would seem that the problem of access is more acute for the female population, particularly in districts dominated by the more conservative Indo-Aryan groups. For example, the differential in male/female literacy rates is highest in Baitadi, Bajhang and Doti districts which are the most inaccessible districts in the sampling. Such a finding was only expected in the context of Nepal's socio-cultural setting where boys are free, encouraged and financially supported to move to locations with better educational facilities whereas girls are prohibited and financially not supported in similar educational endeavors. The sex differential in the literacy rate in Manang district, which is equally remote, was found to be lower indicating, characteristically, the more egalitarian behavior towards women in the Tibeto-Burman group as compared to the Indo-Aryan group.

Table 6.4 Fertility and Family Planning by District, 1991

District	Mean No.of Children Ever Born to Ever Married Women 15-49	Child Survival No	%	Knows of at least one FP device in %	Sample Size
Mountain					
Rasuwa	3.8	3.1	81.6	95.2	239
Manang	3.3	2.7	81.8	68.8	29
Bajhang	3.5	2.4	68.6	88.4	326
Solukhumbu	4.1	3.2	78.0	88.7	314
Dolpa	2.7	2.1	77.8	68.7	69
Hills					
Dhankuta	3.5	3.0	85.7	98.9	286
Ilam	3.6	3.2	88.9	95.7	318
Kavre	3.7	3.0	81.1	95.4	341
Dhading	3.7	2.9	78.4	71.3	290
Baglung	3.1	2.1	67.7	98.6	305
Gorkha	3.2	2.6	81.2	94.1	284
Surkhet	3.8	3.1	81.6	73.5	345
Pyuthan	3.5	2.9	82.9	87.5	329
Doti	3.7	2.9	78.4	74.1	404
Baitadi	3.2	2.6	81.2	68.0	440
Kathmandu	3.0	2.6	86.7	98.1	324
Lalitpur	3.5	2.9	82.8	97.3	291
Bhaktapur	3.7	3.1	83.7	96.6	408
Tarai					
Morang	3.7	3.1	83.8	96.6	408
Sarlahi	3.4	2.6	76.5	99.3	475
Rupandehi	3.4	2.8	82.4	92.1	675
Bardiya	4.0	3.2	80.0	100.0	507
Kanchanpur	3.5	2.9	82.8	98.6	433

Source: NFHS, 1991. Respective District Tables, Volume II.

94

Fig 6.3 Fertility and Family Planning by District, 1991

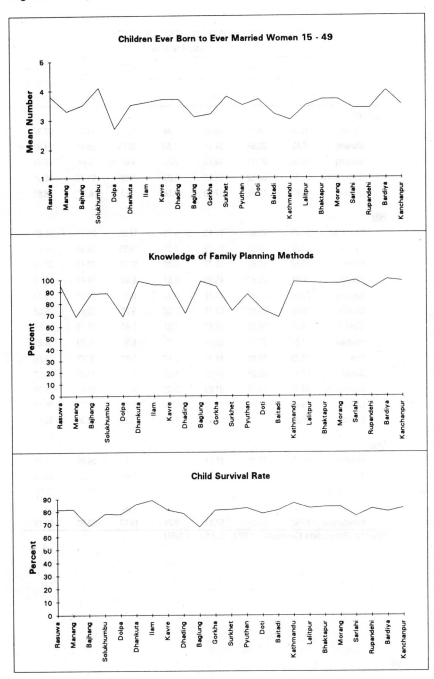

Table 6.5 Literacy Rates by Sex and by District, 1971-91

(Population 6 years and above)

District	Male			Female			Male/Female Difference in 1991
	1971	1981	1991	1971	1981	1991	
Mountain							
Rasuwa	11.36	14.61	33.67	1.36	3.21	11.30	22.37
Manang	7.43	30.59	54.81	1.60	10.19	29.87	24.97*
Bajhang	17.61	20.71	49.85	1.25	4.67	6.94	42.91
Solukhumbu	21.50	34.52	56.33	3.03	8.86	21.32	35.01
Dolpa	8.90	19.35	37.30	1.58	5.13	8.37	28.93
Hills							
Dhankuta	27.75	47.40	65.63	4.70	14.26	33.01	32.62
Ilam	26.87	46.07	65.73	6.01	18.98	38.82	26.91
Kavre	19.68	35.82	55.77	2.70	12.29	23.40	32.37
Dhading	9.38	22.67	45.93	0.87	6.83	18.41	27.52
Baglung	25.91	36.82	56.49	2.72	9.86	27.08	29.41
Gorkha	20.82	27.61	57.15	2.38	9.28	30.87	26.28
Surkhet	19.00	34.22	59.97	1.87	9.69	25.39	34.58
Pyuthan	24.87	27.31	51.14	1.75	6.30	16.89	34.25
Doti	13.25	19.88	48.46	1.17	5.87	9.80	38.66
Baitadi	25.45	32.86	59.52	2.00	8.15	13.35	46.17
Kathmandu	53.75	59.92	81.63	21.22	38.20	56.57	25.06
Lalitpur	39.09	48.15	76.33	10.37	24.60	47.77	28.56
Bhaktapur	40.21	46.12	74.55	7.05	17.83	42.38	32.17
Tarai							
Morang	30.26	40.35	61.84	8.41	19.58	34.99	26.85
Sarlahi	13.68	24.02	37.50	2.43	6.46	13.22	24.28
Rupandehi	26.15	39.93	53.16	5.49	13.94	26.08	27.08
Bardiya	8.36	19.17	41.36	1.96	7.86	16.76	24.60
Kanchanpur	18.62	33.28	57.97	3.24	12.07	22.80	35.17

Source: Population Censuses, 1971, 1981 and 1991

Fig 6.4 Male/Female Differential in Literacy Rate by District

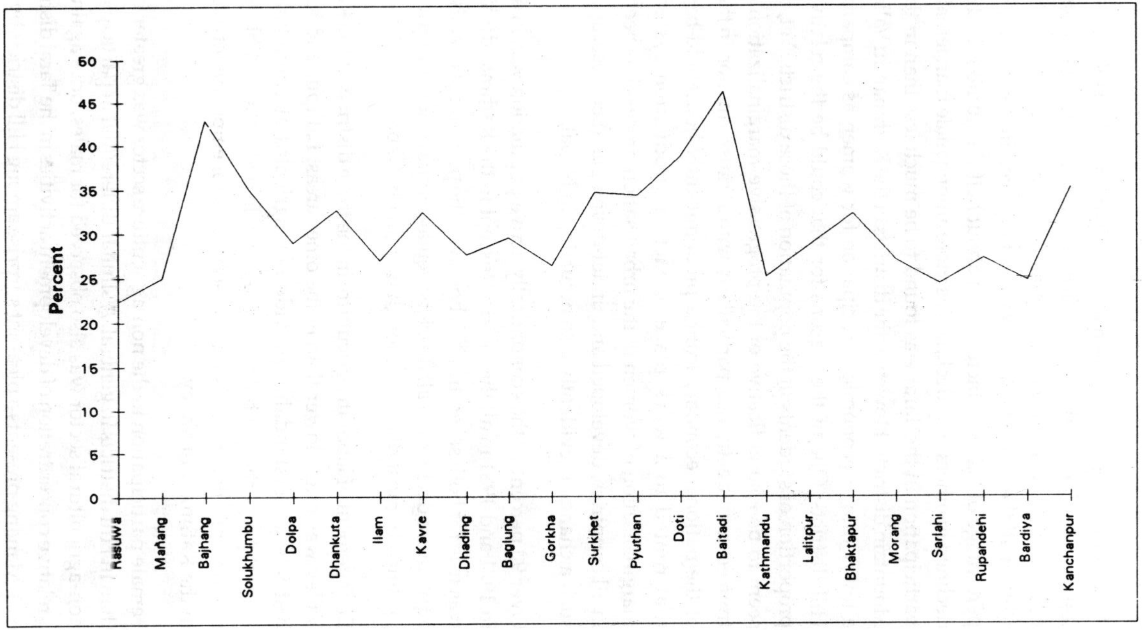

6.5 Labor Force Participation

According to census data, female participation in the labor force is always less than for their male counterparts (Table 6.6). A close observation of the figures in Table 6.6 reveals that male economic activity rates declined in 1991 in all the districts under review. However, in the case of females the percentage of "active" increased in about half the number of districts and declined in others. The decline was more among male than females. Female participation in the Tarai was found to be much less than in the Hill and Mountain districts. However, the districts of the Kathmandu Valley, showed a lower rate of economic participation for women as compared to other Hill districts. One of the reasons for that could be the relatively higher proportion of students in the population of those districts. Yet, that would seem to be also indicative of the progressive marginalization of women from economic activities, particularly with a transformation in the character of the national economy from a predominantly household-based one to that rooted to a work place or factory production system. Such a marginalisation of women in the urbanisation process has been observed in all countries, developed and under-developed (See Boserup, 1970) and such a change is evidently also occurring in Nepal.

Over 90 percent of the economically active population was in agriculture in 1971 and 1981 in all the districts, except in the Kathmandu Valley. That was true for both sexes. In 1991, however, the percentage of active males in agriculture declined in all districts. Female employment in agriculture also declined in most districts, though marginally (Table 6.7).

Engagement of labor in agriculture in the three districts of the Kathmandu Valley was much lower than in the other areas. Lalitpur and Kathmandu districts understandably provide non-agricultural employment to the highest proportion of both male and female population (Table 6.8), due to the concentration of industrial and service sector employment opportunities in the Kathmandu Valley.

Female participation in the non-agriculture sector was greater in the Tarai than in Hill districts in general. A similar differential in participation in the non-agricultural sector was also observed for males, once again reflecting a relative concentration of development activities in the Tarai districts (Table 6.8). Manang presents a pleasant surprise among Hill districts by providing non-agriculture employment to more than 25 percent of the female and 48 percent of the male population. That may probably be attributed to trading activities in that particular district.

Table 6.6 Percent of Economically Active Population
by Sex and by District, 1971-1991 (10 years and above)

District	Male			Female		
	1971	1981	1991	1971	1981	1991
Mountain						
Rasuwa	89.34	89.89	78.89	77.76	53.79	67.62
Manang	74.07	86.40	77.89	45.31	78.40	72.42
Bajhang	84.81	82.63	72.67	67.27	44.08	77.29
Solukhumbu	79.22	85.80	72.69	53.05	77.51	73.66
Dolpa	78.80	95.54	80.20	28.70	96.09	75.02
Hills						
Dhankuta	81.11	80.66	72.53	45.94	53.45	68.99
Ilam	80.43	78.56	67.45	40.51	51.26	51.01
Kavre	87.29	82.01	69.78	63.81	61.25	60.67
Dhading	90.18	85.73	73.25	59.49	60.63	65.14
Baglung	79.93	79.20	59.61	59.72	53.93	55.85
Gorkha	82.56	85.72	63.72	39.97	75.84	60.33
Surkhet	80.42	82.61	66.91	10.70	47.74	44.01
Pyuthan	78.65	87.02	72.74	30.42	71.10	65.40
Doti	82.05	91.01	74.96	33.41	58.16	76.25
Baitadi	81.53	86.57	65.70	52.61	59.68	72.37
Kathmandu	66.94	76.12	59.72	18.04	39.83	28.89
Lalitpur	74.01	78.22	61.76	30.90	36.05	36.44
Bhaktapur	76.52	75.42	63.61	28.85	44.89	45.82
Tarai						
Morang	83.55	79.21	65.18	9.53	37.47	30.66
Sarlahi	87.65	88.24	72.85	14.83	12.12	14.79
Rupandehi	82.53	79.56	65.69	14.30	16.50	26.71
Bardiya	83.63	91.03	68.02	19.81	65.60	32.63
Kanchanpur	88.17	86.02	66.72	11.79	41.26	36.16

Source: Population Censuses, 1971, 1981 and 1991.

Table 6.7 Economically Active Population in Agriculture by Sex and by District, 1971-1991

(Percent in agriculture to total economically active)a/

District	Male			Female		
	1971	1981	1991	1971	1981	1991
Mountain						
Rasuwa	94.1	95.0	84.0	98.4	97.4	96.2
Manang	95.7	74.2	51.3	82.2	93.7	73.6
Bajhang	98.4	96.1	87.3	99.1	99.3	96.9
Solukhumbu	97.9	94.1	83.0	98.9	96.8	95.4
Dolpa	96.3	96.1	85.2	99.0	97.2	96.3
Hills						
Dhankuta	95.9	89.5	82.9	98.2	95.1	94.6
Ilam	95.8	92.4	85.2	98.4	96.1	93.8
Kavre	95.2	91.2	83.2	99.3	96.1	95.9
Dhading	98.5	93.3	87.1	99.7	96.4	96.7
Baglung	95.5	93.9	86.3	99.4	97.8	97.2
Gorkha	97.1	95.1	86.2	99.5	98.1	96.8
Surkhet	97.4	92.6	79.7	99.2	96.9	92.8
Pyuthan	96.0	95.2	86.8	99.4	98.8	98.0
Doti	98.2	96.1	81.7	99.2	98.6	96.8
Baitadi	96.0	95.7	85.9	99.4	98.2	98.6
Kathmandu	47.5	65.3	17.7	76.8	86.7	43.8
Lalitpur	66.9	74.3	33.9	90.1	90.5	61.9
Bhaktapur	67.5	75.9	51.3	88.1	91.1	83.4
Tarai						
Morang	80.0	77.9	54.5	87.9	89.6	69.9
Sarlahi	94.3	84.9	78.1	96.2	91.4	80.3
Rupandehi	91.1	84.4	73.0	96.4	92.0	86.4
Bardiya	97.4	96.2	79.7	98.9	98.8	90.0
Kanchanpur	96.5	93.6	80.6	98.8	98.7	93.1

Source: Population Censuses, 1971, 1981 and 1991.

a/ Agriculture and Non-Agriculture do not add up to 100 because of the omission of the not stated category.

Fig 6.5 Percent of Economically Active Female Population by District, 1991

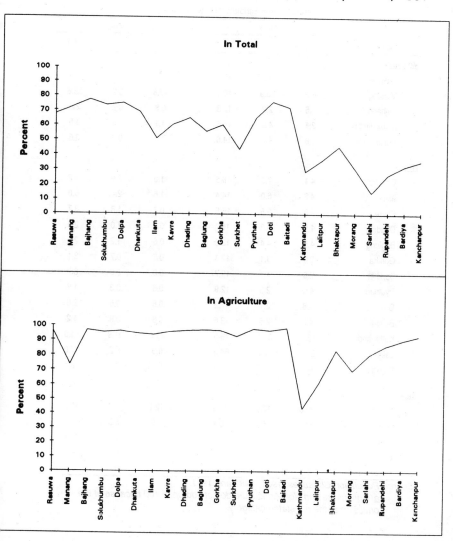

Table 6.8 Economically Active Population in Non-Agricultural
Sectors by Sex and by District, 1971-1991
(Percent of non-agricultural to total active)a/

District	Male			Female		
	1971	1981	1991	1971	1981	1991
Mountain						
Rasuwa	5.9	3.2	15.4	1.6	1.1	3.6
Manang	4.3	23.9	48.4	17.8	5.2	25.6
Bajhang	1.6	2.2	12.3	0.9	0.2	2.8
Solukhumbu	2.1	4.2	16.5	1.1	1.8	4.5
Dolpa	3.8	1.2	14.6	1.0	0.2	3.6
Hills						
Dhankuta	4.1	7.9	16.5	1.8	2.9	5.2
Ilam	4.2	6.0	14.4	1.6	2.4	6.0
Kavre	4.8	6.5	15.5	0.7	1.8	3.7
Dhading	1.5	3.3	11.7	0.3	1.0	2.9
Baglung	4.5	4.4	13.0	0.6	1.2	2.5
Gorkha	2.9	3.1	13.4	0.5	0.7	3.1
Surkhet	2.6	4.7	19.7	0.8	2.0	6.9
Pyuthan	4.0	2.3	12.9	0.6	0.3	1.9
Doti	1.8	2.1	17.2	0.8	0.5	2.6
Baitadi	4.0	2.5	13.6	0.6	0.8	1.2
Kathmandu	52.5	31.1	78.5	23.2	11.9	54.0
Lalitpur	33.1	22.8	64.0	9.9	8.2	37.0
Bhaktapur	32.5	21.5	46.9	11.9	7.1	16.1
Tarai						
Morang	20.0	17.9	42.5	12.1	6.7	28.2
Sarlahi	5.7	14.3	20.4	3.8	8.3	18.3
Rupandehi	8.9	13.8	25.9	3.6	7.0	13.0
Bardiya	2.6	2.6	19.2	1.1	0.7	9.0
Kanchanpur	3.5	4.6	18.3	1.2	0.8	6.3

Source: Population Censuses, 1971, 1981 and 1991.
a/ Agriculture and Non-Agriculture do not add up to 100 because of the omission of the not stated category.

In conclusion, there are indications of a changing demographic profile connected to their level of development in the districts surveyed. One such indicator is level of literacy. The more developed the district, the higher the female literacy rate, although socio-economic factors do play a significant role in the relative literacy status of the female population. The differential in male/female literacy rates besides reflecting socio-cultural attitudes vis-a-vis female education also reflects the availability or non-availability of educational opportunities. On the other hand, with the process of development women are being marginalized from economic arena with their economic participation rates varying inversely with the level of development of the district. The Tarai districts generally recorded lower economic activity rates for women. A large proportion of households in Tarai communities practice female seclusion. As such, economic activities by women are not always reported even if they work in their family fields as strenuously as their menfolks (see Acharya, 1981). Only when women are pushed out to wage labor, they are reported as economically active. In the Tarai districts the mix of Hill and Tarai communities would also effect the reported economic activity rates as women from the hill communities show higher probability of reporting their activities correctly. It is notable that Morang (the more industrialised district on the one hand, and Bardiya and Kanchanpur with large proportion of hill people resettled in last 20 years) on the other, report higher economic activity rates for women.

VII. POLITICAL PARTICIPATION AND ACCESS TO POSITIONS OF POWER

7.1 Political Positions

Political participation by women may be assessed within a two-dimensional framework: participation in mass political movements in times of crisis and sustained political activities through time and rise to positions of power. Although in times of crisis women have been mobilized to participate in mass political movements in Nepal (e.g. in 1951 and 1990) as in other countries in the region (Manikkymaba, 1986, Chowdhari, 1994, Feijoo, 1994) their involvement has been sporadic which is to say not sustained through time. Consequently, few women have climbed to positions of power in the country.

The basic features of the dominant Indo-Aryan culture, the patrilineal inheritance system and extreme concern over the purity of the female body discourage and hinder women from political participation. The patrilineal inheritance system, which makes women's access to property conditional on her martial behavior and status, severely limit her ability to use such resources either for political purposes or for her individual advancement. The excessive concern of the Indo-Aryan community with clan purity and, consequently, with the purity of the female body greatly restrict women's mobility as adolescents and young women. The combined impact of these two factors has tended to keep women away from the public domain and thus reduce her access to knowledge, education and positions of power. (For a detailed discussion of these issues see Acharya, 1994). The political changes of 1990 which ushered in a democratic system of governance in the country, may make a difference to women's political participation and access to positions of power in a long term perspective. In the short term, however, no change on that score is visible. Today, there are fewer women in positions of political power than under the previous system. Thus, in all cabinets formed during the Panchayat era there was at least one woman minister. One woman was included in the first cabinet formed by a democratically elected parliament in 1991. However, she had to resign shortly after her induction due to differences with the prime minister. Currently, there is no woman in the cabinet.

The new democratic constitution, promulgated in 1990, makes it mandatory for all political parties to propose a minimum 5 percent of women candidates in general elections for parliament. In the 1991 general elections no political party put up significantly more than 5 percent women candidates. Women candidates also complained that they were fielded in the more difficult constituencies. (Personal communication). This is also corroborated by the fact that a lower proportin of women condidates were successul in winning the election when compered to their male counterparts.

The Lower House, or House of Representatives, presently has 7 women (3.4 percent) among 205 members. That is proportionately considerably lower than the corresponding figure in the last National Panchayat (Table 7.1). Altogether, 81 women candidates contested for the seats in the House of Representative. Of this a mere 8.6 percent won their elections. The corresponding figure for males was 15.7 percent (Table 7.2). Of the 140 National Panchayat members in 1990, 5.7 percent were women. Of those, 109 men and 3 women were elected; the rest were nominated by the King. About 4.6 percent of all candidates contesting in the last election for the National Panchayat were women. Only three, i.e. 4.5 percent, of female candidates won. That corresponded to a success rate for their male counterparts of about eight percent (Table 7.2).

The next important echelon in the political power structure are locally elected bodies such as municipalities, village development and district development committees. Of the 75 chairpersons of district development committees none is a woman. There is only one woman who serves as vice-chairperson at the district level. Two thousand one hundred and twelve men and seven women had contested elections for district development committee membership. Six women and 1068 men were successful. The high success rate of female candidates is explained by their small number.

Under the Panchayat system local bodies were known as local Panchayats. There were 75 district panchayat executive committees in the country, with 825 elected positions, including chair and vice-chairpersons. In the last District Panchayats, only five women were elected. Fifteen women had contested for the district level membership where only five, i.e. 33 percent, were successful, compared to an overall success rate of 22 percent for men. Thus, as at the present, no woman has been elected to position of chairperson of a district body.

In 1990/91 of the 35,883 village development committee members only 210, i.e. 0.58 percent, were women. Among candidates for those elections 0.9 percent comprised women. Of all elected village development committee chairpersons, women constitute 0.45 percent. In the municipalities, too, the picture is not much different. Those figures do not vary greatly from the village or town panchayats of 1986-87 (Table 7.1).

Table 7.1 Women Among Various Levels of Political Institutions

(Persons)

Post	1991 a/		1986/87 Panchayats	
	Women	Total	Women	Total
Village Development Committee Chairpersons	11 (0.28)	3993	12 (0.30)	4012
Village Development Committee Vice-chairpersons	18 (0.45)	3993	7 (0.17)	4005
Village Development Committee Members	210 (0.58)	35883	1060 (0.59)	179480
Municipality Mayors	0	36	0	31
Municipality Deputy Mayors	0	36	1 (3.22)	31
Municipality Members	2 (0.38)	521	4 (0.91)	439
District Development Committee Chairperson	0	75	0	75
District Development Committee Vice-Chairperson	1 (1.33)	75	0	75
District Development Committee Members	6 (0.65)	924	5 (0.74)	675
Members of the House of Representatives	7 (3.41)	205	8 (5.7)	104
Total	255 (0.56)	45741	1097 (0.58)	188963

Source: Compiled from Election Reports published by the Election Commission for respective elections.

a/   Several posts were vacant as Elections to 77 positions at the village level and 3 positions at the districts level were either disturbed or postponed due to various reasons.

Note: Figures within parentheses indicate percentage to the total number of persons in each category.

Fig. 7.1 Women Among Levsls of Political Institutions

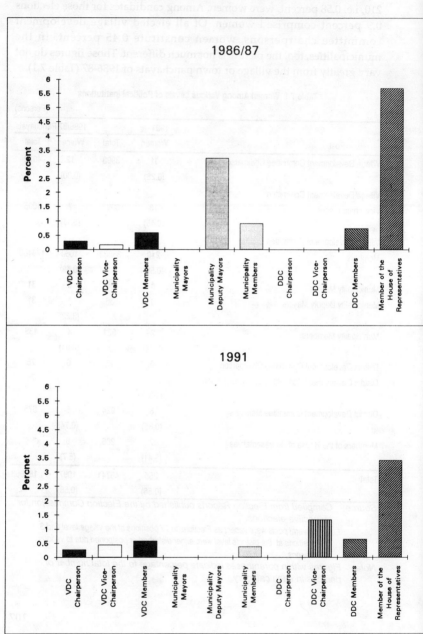

Thus, women constituted a slightly higher proportion (0.9 percent) among district and village level candidates in the 1991 elections for local government institutions compared to 1986/87 (see Table 7.2) when only 0.5 percent of all the candidates for district and village panchayats were women. However, at the village level, a much lower proportion was elected, as compared to 1986/87, while at the district level the proportion of women who were successful was considerably higher. Overall, there has been little change in the relative access of women to positions of political power.

Table 7.2 Male/Female Participation as Candidates in Election.

(Persons)

Institutions	1991 a/			1986/87 (Panchayats)		
	Male	Female	Total	Male	Female	Total
House of Representative						
a) Candidates	1264	81	1345	1401	67	1468
b) Elected	197	7	205	109	3	112
c) Percent elected	15.7	8.6	15.2	7.8	4.5	7.6
District Development Committee						
a) Candidates	2112	7	2119	3688	15	3673
b) Elected	1068	6	1074	820	5	825
c) Percent elected	50.6	85.7	50.7	22.2	33.3	22.5
Village Development Committee/ Municipality						
a) Candidates	101546	956	102502	272777	1423	274200
b) Elected	44221	241	44462	187485	1079	188564
c) Percent elected	43.5	25.2	43.4	68.7	75.8	68.8

Source: Compiled from Election Reports published by the Election Commission for respective elections.

a/ Several posts were vacant as Elections to 77 positions at the village level and 3 positions at the districts level were either disturbed or postponed due to various reasons.

7.2 Administration

Women's access to the decision making process can also be gleaned from their access to the higher echelons of the bureaucracy. On this front, too, Nepalese women lag far behind their menfolks. This gender disparity in access to decision making roles has not been decreasing in any perceptive manner. Occupationally, the proportion of women in the category of professional and technical workers has declined to 15.1 percent in 1991 compared to 16.6 percent in 1981. The proportion of women in public administration has, however, been increasing steadily since 1971, from 4.2 percent that year to 6.6 percent in 1981 and 9.3 percent in 1991 (see Table 4.10).

A more detailed, position-by-position comparison of government employment figures, as of July 1978 and July 1993, also indicate increasing participation of women in public administration as officers (Table 7.3). Yet, as of July 1994, there are still no women at the highest level of the bureaucracy: officers of the "special class". At the lower levels, women's participation, though still less than five percent, is on the increase.

Similarly, the proportion of female personnel in selected government agencies and semi-government corporations has increased from 8.9 percent in 1978 to 11.7 percent in 1993. Women are concentrated proportionatly more at the level of non gazetted level. (Tables 7.4 and 7.5). That may indicate increasing inability of women to contest for higher level civil service positions due to greater competition from men for the same.

Table 7.3 Proportion of Women in the Government Administration
(July 1978 & July 1993)

	1978			1993		
	Number		Percent of	Number		Percent of
	Total	Female	Women in Total	Total	Female	Women in Total
Gazetted	6099	197	3.23	11232	493	4.39
Special	45	-	-	41	-	-
First Class	353	4	1.13	650	16	2.46
Second Class	1326	33	2.49	3103	139	4.48
Third Class	4375	160	3.66	7438	338	4.54

Source: Nijamati Kitabkhana, HMG.

Table 7.4 Number of Women in Selected Government and Semi-government Institutions
(July 1978 - July 1993)

Institutions Level	Financial a/				Cultural b/				Other c/				Total for Selected Institutions			
	1978		1993		1978		1993		1978		1993		1978		1993	
	Total	Female	Total	Female	Total	Female	Total	Female	Total	Female	Total	Female	Total	Female	Total	Female
Gazetted	1308	88	536	49	40	5	13	5	841	43	1294	128	2189	136	1843	182
Non-Gazetted	7396	967	3015	404	163	32	12	7	5042	381	8490	1122	12601	1380	11517	1533
Support Staff	2249	111	674	44	40	2	7	0	1799	53	3788	335	4088	166	4469	379
Total	**1(953**	**1166**	**4225**	**497**	**243**	**39**	**32**	**12**	**7682**	**477**	**13572**	**1585**	**18878**	**1682**	**17829**	**2094**

Table 7.5 Proportion of Women in Selected Government and Semi-government Institutions
(July 1978 - July 1993)

(Percent of Women in Total)

Institutions Level	Financial a/		Cultural b/		Others c/		Total	
	1978	1993	1978	1993	1978	1993	1978	1993
Gazetted	6.73	9.14	12.50	38.46	5.11	9.89	6.21	9.88
Non-Gazetted	13.07	13.40	19.63	58.33	7.56	13.22	10.95	13.31
Support Staff	4.94	6.53	5.00	-	2.95	8.84	4.06	8.48
Total	**10.65**	**11.76**	**16.50**	**37.50**	**6.21**	**11.68**	**8.91**	**11.74**

Source: Respective Corporations:
a/ includes: Nepal Rastra Bank*, Two Commercial Banks, Life Insurance Company*, Provident Fund Corporation*, Industrial Development Corporation*, Agricultural Development Bank and Credit Guarantee Corporation*.
b/ includes: Cultural Corporation* and Royal Nepal Film Corporation (The two have been merged).
c/ includes: National Trading Ltd. Central Office*, Agricultural Inputs Corporation, Nepal Food Corporation*, Dairy Development Corporation, Banshbari Shoe Factory, Royal Drug Ltd.*, and Himal Cement Company, Electricity Corporation*, Tele-Communication Corporation of Nepal*, Oil Corporation* and Royal Nepal Airlines Corporation.

* In above notes indicate corporations included in 1993 data.

Five women leaders - Determined to change the women's world.

Learning tc lead.

VIII. GENDER PERSPECTIVE IN POPULATION POLICIES

8.1 Population Policies

Although family planning (FP) had been incorporated in government policy in Nepal since 1965, only the Fifth Five Year Plan (1975/76-1979/80) spelt out official population policy in any detail. The entire thrust in earlier plans was focused on family planning alone. The fifth plan, for the very first time, shifted that emphasis to providing Maternal and Child Health (MCH) services and thus outlined its objectives: "To reduce birth rate directly through preventive programs such as maternal and child health and family planning and indirectly by improving the socio-economic conditions as well as cultural and educational levels of the population." (Fifth Plan, Nepali, p. 42).

A full blown chapter on population with objectives, policies, priorities and programs was included only in the Sixth Five Year Plan (1980/81-1984/85). The two objectives outlined in the plan were to stabilize the population growth rate around 2.3 percent per annum and to regularize the internal and external migration process. Increasing the coverage and effectiveness of FP programs topped the list of priorities. Integration of FP programs with other development activities and mobilization of people's participation in FP programs were envisaged for the first time. Women and women's programs also featured for the first time in population policy. A more comprehensive and multi-dimensional approach to population control, which included extensive integration of population education in various formal and non-formal educational programs was outlined.

The Seventh Five Year Plan (1985/86 - 1989/90) and, currently, the Eighth Five Year Plan (1991/92 - 1996/97) further elaborate on the objectives, priorities, policies and programs in the same direction. Total fertility rate is targeted to be reduced to 4.5 by the end of the Eighth Plan period. The goals set on the health front are outlined comprehensively in Table 8.1. Programs for female education and improvement in women's status have been specially mentioned (Table 8.2). The objective and policies on women and children have been outlined in separate chapters in two recent Plans and these have been summarized in Tables 8.3 and 8.4 below. A comparative analysis of these two plans show very little change in the approach to population or women's issues.

Table 8.1: NEPAL GOALS FOR THE 1990s

Indicator	NEPAL Current Situation 1990	Goals 1996	Goals 2001	Global Goals for 2000
Health and Sanitation				
Infant Mortality per 1,000 live births	107	80	50	50 per 1,000 or 1/3 of the current rate, whichever is less
Under-Five Mortality per 1,000 live births	165	130	70	70 per 1,000 or 1/3 of the current rate, whichever is less
Maternal Mortality per 100 thousand births	850	750	400	By 1/2
Annual Cases Prevented				
Poliomyelitis	9,323	11,122	Eradication	Eradication
Neonatal Tetanus	17,021	20,776	Elimination by 1995	Eradication by 1995
Measles	391,962	467,510	To reduce measles mortality by 95% and morbidity by 90% by 1995	Reduction of measles death by 95% & measles morbidity cases 90% by 1995
Levels (Percent)				
Malnutrition	50	44	25	Reduction by 1/2
Iron deficiency-anaemia	78	70	50	Reduction by 1/3
Vitamin A deficiency & its consequences including blindness	2.1	1.5	0.1	Virtual elimination
Iodine deficiency disorders	40	28	1	Virtual elimination
Access to Safe Drinking Water	Rural:35 Urban:66 Total:37	50 75 53	75 90 77	Universal access
Access to sanitary means of excreta-disposal	Rural: 3 Urban:34 Total: 6	12 50 16	25 75 31	Universal access
Education (Percent)				
Net enrollment Primary age group	Total :64 Female:31	80 65	100 100	Universal access
Completion of primary education	27	55	70 and above	By at least 80% of primary school age children
Adult Illiteracy	Total: 65 Female:82	51 67	32 41	Reduction to at least half, with emphasis on female literacy

Source: UNICEF, Children and Women of Nepal: A Situation Analysis, 1992.

Table 8.2: Seventh and Eighth Five Year Plan:
Policies outlined to Achieve the Population Goals

7th Plan (1985/86-1989/90)

1. to fulfill the unmet deamd in family planning services by rapidly expanding service outlets.

2. to integrae population programs in development programs.

3. To involve local panchayats, class organizations and other non-government organizations in population activities.

4. To regularzie the increasing migration.

5. to emphasize women's development programs.

Specifically

a) Female participation in formal and non-formal education, skill trainings and trade schools, and higher education will be encouraged by providing incentives and opportunities.

b) Attempts will be made to increase opportunities for women's employment in specific sectors.

8th Plan 1992/93-1996/97

1. To increase consciousness for small families by creating congenial economic atmosphere for 2-children families.

2. To integrate family planning programs with primary health.

3. To increase the participation of non-government and private sectors in supply of FP services.

4. To increase skilled human resources by training and education.

5. To develop female education programs to improve women's social and economic status.

Specifically

Program's for female education, skill development and employment will be conducted with special emphasis.

117

Table 8.3: Seventh and Eighth Five Year Plan:
Policy Declarations on Women and Development

The Seventh Plan (1985/86 - 1989/90)

1. To enable women to participate activity in the development process by providing appropriate opportunities, to foster self-reliance among women by increasing their productive capacity and to raise their social and economic status by this all round development.

2. There will be additional programs for women in the field of agricultural extension. Quotas will be fixed in various training programs.

3. Training on basic health needs and maternal and childcare programs will be conducted.

4. Literacy among women will be increased. In the education sector, quotas and special incentives will be used to increase female participation in education and various training programs.

5. More emphasis will be given to development of cottage industries for providing work for women during the off-agricultural seasons. Special provision will be made for women in the provision of training facilities, credit and other resources. Marketing facilities will also be developed.

6. Women will be encouraged to get involved in forest protection and preservation.

7. Facilities will be provided for participation in government and non-government organizations.

8. Legal reforms will be effected to remove provisions hindering women's participation in national development.

9. Nepal Women's Organization will be facilitated to conduct development activities for women.

The Eighth Plan (1992/93 - 1996/97)

1. The Government is committed to equal and meaningful participation of women in development process.

2. Programs designed to enhance women's participation will be included in economic and social sectors (agriculture, forestry, industry, health & education)

3. Policies will also be enunciated to raise employment opportunities for women in these areas.

4. Credit, technical know-how, entrepreneurship training & market services will be extended.

5. Policies will be adopted to encourage the appointment of women in the government, semi-government & non-government sectors and to provide them opportunities for career development.

6. Laws and by laws which hinder the development of women will be reformed.

7. Information on gender discrimination at work will be monitored and documented.

8. A suitable organizational structure will be formed for coordination and monitoring activities relating to women.

Table 8.4: Seventh and Eighth Five Year Plan:
Policies on Children's Development

Seventh Plan (1985/86-1989/90)

1. To educate parents about nutrition, education and general child raring principles.
2. To expand nutrition programs for pregnant and lactating mothers in rural areas.
3. To expand coverage of various vaccinations for 0-5 age children and to increase their effectiveness.
4. To supply the minimum necessary medicines including Jeevan Jal for children in local health posts.
5. To supply nutritions food for children at reasonable prices.
6. To expand the referral facilities for children.
7. To expand the number of primary schools and distribution of free textbooks.
8. To establish day-care centres in urban locations with concentration of women workers (e.g. factories).
9. To organize sportive and cultural events, publish books and reading materials libraries, sport clubs and make movies for children.
10. To help the disabled children to gain self-confidence by giving them opportunities for education and skill development.
11. To carry out these programs in an integrated framework.
12. To involve non-government organizations in the above activities.

Eighth Plan (1992/93-1996/97

1. To expand provision of maternal and child health facilities in the rural areas.
2. To expand immunization and child health education programs.
3. To improve the nutritional status of children by coordination of health education and employment programs and promotion of nutrition programs at the sub-health post level.
4. To expand pediatric health services by strengthening facilities for children in hospitals.
5. To encourage small family norms through family planning services.
6. To establish day-care centres and pre-primary schools with involvement of local government and non-government institutions.
7. To provide free primary education, improve the quality and quantity of primary education and increase female enrollment through various incentives.
8. To facilitate secondary level and vocational education.
9. To launch special programs for working children and children in diffident circumstances (abandoned, orphaned street children drug abusers etc.), through encouragement to national and international NGOs.
10. To encourage NGO's to assist the government in the effective implementation of the laws on children's rights.
11. To encourage and help local institutions to incorporate targets and goals on children in their development plans and programs.
12. To create a high level National Children Development Council including representation from NGOs to co-ordinate and monitor the execution of the child development programs.

119

In summary, population programs in Nepal have evolved through several stages conforming to international trends. Initially, population programs were limited to FP. Then MCH was introduced. Currently, the complexity of the population problem is viewed in a broader framework and related to infant mortality and child survival rates, women's education and employment. However, women's health needs are still perceived only as a MCH problem.

8.2 An Evaluation: from a gender perspective

The changes in population policy towards a more integratd FP, MCH and health services are, no doubt an improvement over the one sided emphasis on family planning. From a gender perspective the following elements in the population policies are definitely positive:

a) Concern expressed for maternal health and attempts to integrate health and family planning programs even though limited to only mother and child health. That should assist in improving women's lives since maternal mortality is still quite high. The risk of death from pregnancy-related causes is still about 1 in 31 (NFHS, p. 145).

b) Intended integration of FP services in development programs could increase the effectiveness of family planning messages significantly. However, little attention has been paid to implementation of such a policy, thus far. Attempts to integrate income generating activities for women by FP agencies have failed because they were conceptualized without any attention to economic viability or sustainability (e.g. various population education programs implemented during the eighties. See Acharya, 1989).

c) Emphasis on the education of the female child and delay in marriage — both enhance women's life options and help to reduce the fertility rate.

However, there are several other elements in proposed policies which are of some concern for women activists:

a) The Government has greatly emphasized the involvement of local government institutions in population programs. It is not clear how such involvement will increase the effectiveness of population programs as the leadership at this level is not itself convinced about the soundness of such programs. Without a concerted effort to generate such an awareness at the local leadership level, its involvement in any

FP program may only hinder progress. Even today, few FP cadre themselves are required to practice what they preach. Currently even the Village Health Workers (VHW) do not visit households regularly, nor are women aware of such visits (Table 8.5). The provision of MCH workers at the sub-health post level, as is envisaged in the new public health structure, is a welcome move. However, such positions may be difficult to be filled unless all-out efforts are made to, recruit, train and retain them in those positions. A large proportion of ANM positions even in district hospitals are often vacant (see MOH, 1991).

Table 8.5: Womens's Knowledge of and Visit by VHW

Category	Percent
Don't know VHW	63.0
Never Visited	46.8
Visited Last month	14.8
Visited 1-2 month	22.8
Visited 3-5 month	*6.8*

Source: NFHS 1991 Table 9.15

b) Although integration of FP education in school and adult literacy text books has been attempted, such texts are still gender biased, emphasizing only the role of mothers and wives. Scant attention is paid to women as "women".

c) Although formulation of policy on children and women in itself marks some achievement, the crux of the matter lies in its implementation. Most sectoral policies and programs even today ignore women or plan for only their token involvement e.g. in agriculture training, community forestry programs, etc.

d) Population is one issue where women's role is over emphasized. Data is collected on women's fertility and not on how many children a father shires. Given the incidence of extensive polygamy, that is an important factor in itself, even if the issue of women's reproductive rights are ignored. Although women are less mobile and have less access to resources concentrated in urban areas than men, the burden of adopting family planning methods in mostly placed on them. It has also been found that women may be rejected if they practice family planning without the consent of their husbands (see Lakhey & Malla, 1992).

A review of statistics on the use of contraceptives reveals that there has been an excessive emphasis on female sterilization in recent years. From 1981 to 1991, for instance, the number of female sterilizations increased more than 358 percent while the male sterilization rate increased merely by 134 percent (Table 8.6).

Table 8.6 : Trends in Ever Use of Contraceptives
(Percent of Currently Married Women)

Contraceptive Method	Who have Ever Used			
	1976	1981	1986	1991
Any Modern Method	**3.7**	**8.6**	**15.8**	**26.7**
Female Sterilisation	0.1	2.4	6.2	11.0
Male Sterilisation	1.5	2.9	5.7	6.8
Pill	1.9	3.1	1.8	5.4
Injection	-	0.4	0.6	4.6
Condom	1.2	1.2	1.2	2.3
Norplant	-	-	-	0.3
IUD	0.2	0.2	0.2	0.6
Diaphragm, Foam, Jelly	-	-	-	0.4

Source: a/ Nepal Fertility Survey, 1976
b/ Nepal Fertility and Family Planning Survey Report, 1986.
c/ Nepal Fertility, Family Planning and Health Survey, 1991.

e)   Most family planning devices are targeted on women without much attention to their side effects. In a recent NFH Survey (1991) more than 18 percent of women not using FP devices expressed health concerns and side effects as the factors for their non-use (Table 8.7). For poor women who have no access to resources for treatment in case of failure, it is undoubtedly risky to accept family planning methods.

f)   Women's non-maternity related health needs are ignored. In a society where infertility is a curse, provision of fertility control service, by itself, is not adequate. In the NHF survey over 18 percent women were reported infertile or menopausal by the time they were between 30-34 years of age (p. 79). Women have no security if her fertility system fails. As a married woman, she has no property rights in her natal household and her status in the affinal household is jeopardized if abandoned by the husband. According to Nepal's Muluki Ain (Law of the Land, clause 9) husbands are permitted to remarry on any of the following conditions:

- If the wife is mentally ill with no possibility of cure;

- If the wife has an infectious or incurable venereal disease;

- If the wife is living separate, having acquired her share of the family "ansa";

- If the wife is an invalid and cannot move;

- If she is blind in both the eyes; and

- If she has no "child" even after ten years of marriage. (Earlier the condition stipulated "son" rather than "child"). Currently, socially it is interpreted as "son" even if legally it says "child".

Table 8.7: Reason for Non-use of Family Planning

Reason for Non-use (present)	Respondent's Age		Total
	<30	30+	
Wants children	69.4	16.8	37.8
Lack of knowledge	5.3	5.3	5.3
Partner opposed	2.8	4.2	3.6
Cost too much	0.1	0.1	0.1
Side effects	8.8	15.5	12.8
Health concerns	2.1	7.9	5.6
Hard to get methods	0.2	0.5	0.4
Religion	4.3	5.6	5.0
Opposed to FP	0.9	1.5	1.2
Fatalistic	0.7	0.4	0.5
Other people opposed	0.3	0.2	1.2
Infrequent sex	1.9	2.4	0.5
Difficult to be preg.	0.7	17.1	0.3
Menopausal, had hyst.	0.1	20.7	2.2
Inconvenient	0.6	0.6	10.6
Don't know	1.9	1.1	12.4
Missing	0.0	0.1	0.6
Total : Percent	**100.0**	**100.0**	**100.0**
Number	**3,466**	**5,212**	**8,678**

Source: NFHS. 1991 Table 9.22

g) Women's reproductive organs are infected by various venereal diseases and, now, by AIDS. No health education or facilities are available for their treatment. Infections are often caused by a philandering husband. However, it is women who are often blamed and abandoned. Cervical cancer, which is becoming a major problem in Nepal, is induced by the continuous presence of venereal diseases. Very few rural women are aware of that. In Kathmandu and Pokhara, women with venereal diseases are 10 times more than in other towns. Nepal has less than 20 doctors specialized in venereal diseases. (Dixit, 1992). Women, who are socially blamed for these diseases, therefore feel embarrassed to obtain medical treatment, which, of course, only aggravates the situation. AIDS might gain epidemic proportions in the next few years and women's health situation may further deteriorate as people with venereal diseases are specially vulnerable to AIDS. Even the ordinary infection of the urinary tract, which is rampant, is not treated. Use of condoms, which could act as effective protection, is now relegated to the bottom of the priority list as far as FP devices go.

h) Women have very little reproductive rights e.g. with respect to the desired number of children, in selection of marriage partners, and/or deciding the time of marriage. All that is controlled by society. The State reinforces that control by various means. The most glaring éxample of such state induced reinforcement is the fact that irrespective of its causes abortion is considered a crime in Nepal. A bill is expected in the House of Representatives in this summer session (July - August, 1994) proposing some amendments to Muluki Ain. If passed the law will allow abortion on medical grounds within first 12 weeks of pregnancy. Those amendments have been proposed because a large number of women die on account of abortion-related cases. For example, Maskey and Malla (1991) report that septic abortions account for more than 33 percent of maternal mortality in Nepal. Some of those abortions could have been related to the failure of birth control measures. The methods of abortion practiced are often crude — such as injecting a foreign body into the genital track, injury to the genital track, use of paste, cowdung, accreflam solution, etc — and result in a high rate of death. Experts have written that "dangers of illegal abortions can be up to 100 times as great as those of legal abortions" (Ibid). As far back as 1975, those concerns were raised by medical experts. Only now some serious attention is being paid by the authorities to legalizing abortion at the hospital/clinical levels.

Government hospitals and clinics need the husband's consent even for adoption of FP methods. As discussed above, the Law of the Land (Muluki Ain) allows a second marriage for men if no child is born in ten years. Legally, men have the sole right over the children.

If a girl wishes to go abroad for further studies and applies for Government scholarship, she has first to obtain her parents' consent.

i) Adolescent girls have no access to health education or medical services to deal with their problems. The beginning of menarche, even among the urban elite, is viewed with alarm (See Asmita; 1992). Girls view it as a curse or as punishment for sins they may have committed. Culturally, menstrual blood is viewed as impure and rituals related to first menarche frighten them. Sex education is still taboo. Thus, the process of the blooming of a girl's body, which should be perceived as a boon, is viewed with distaste. What irony that the natural process on which the reproduction of the human race is dependent should be viewed as a curse for women! Further, many physical and psychological problems related to the start of menarche are completely ignored in the medical system.

j) The Government media is not adequately used for raising women's issues. Their sole purpose seems to be to make profit besides covering the activities of the party in power. As a consequence, the frequency of programs and advertisements featuring the female body as a commodity is on the rise. All cinemas and stories emphasize the adolescent love relationship, idealizing women's role either as housewives or as "play objects" for the male. Development agencies have to pay for disseminating their programs in the official media with the consequence that only very few developmental messages get into the media. There is a preponderance of pro-natal stories in religious citations. No attempt is made to counteract them by the public media. There in an abundance of non-mother/wife roles in various religious texts. They could be used to propagate women's non-mother/wife roles. However, no such attempts are visible.

k) Finally, there is no group-specific orientation in family planning programming, e.g. how to convince the labor class that vasectomy does not either weaken physical abilities such as load-carrying or cause other illnesses. In my personal observation and personal interviews with people working in Kathmandu, there seems to be a pervasive belief of that sort among the rural/urban labor class. No statistics are compiled on fertility or adoption of FP methods, or other vital statistics according to class in order that appropriate interventions could be devised. That might, in any case, be a more important differentiating variable effecting adoption of FP methods than either ethnicity or geography.

Children (males) are viewed as a resource rather than a liability among the poor as there is little investment in children in such households. They begin earning when they are as young as 6 years of age. That influences child preference in the labor class.

Thus, women's stake on producing sons is high as access to social status and property is through male progeny. Very few other avenues are open to women to gain social status. Infertile or women with only daughters are doomed, even in urban areas. Sons are required to obtain salvation in the after-life, or to dispatch for recruitment into the army for gainful employment, etc. No legal changes have been affected for women to ensure either their independent existence or access to resources during old age. Nepalese women become destitute if divorced or rejected by their husbands. All suggestions to improve their property status have been stonewalled thus far.

It is understood that change in laws to ensure a woman's equal property rights in her natal household will take time. Accordingly, it was recommended that women be ensured access to new "assets" to be created by the Government (Acharya and Bennett, 1981, p. 316-317). One such asset to be created over the next few years is the community or lease forests. If sole entry into the community and lease forests to households could be provided through women's representation that would be a breakthrough. That idea is not implausible as exemplified by the functioning of various community forestry groups in Nepal (for a summary review, see Acharya, 1993) as well as by women's-only representation in Grameen Bank credit groups in Bangladesh. Such a proposal should be given serious consideration, because:

- ☐ Women are more permanently entrenched in rural areas than men who are more mobile. Hence, their participation would be more effective than men's.

- ☐ Women are more closely related to the issue of forest resource use as it is they who are affected the most in terms of time spent to procure water, fuel and fodder for their households.

- ☐ Women lack other assets. As such, they can be expected to guard more passionately than men such an asset.

This idea should not be rejected offhand because of the presumed impractibility derived from a middle-class, gender-biased mentality. To begin with, it could be attempted in a number of Village Development Committees (VDCs) or communities. It could be catalytic for raising women's status in the social psyche without making much of a difference to the access of various households to forest resources.

To conclude, although some attitudinal changes have taken place in population policies, they are still conceptualized in terms of population control and not in terms of "reproductive health." The "reproductive health" approach implies an attitudinal change in population policies from public health oriented Maternal and Child Health (MCH) programs to more integrated packages which would include care for men, women and adolescents' total reproductive health needs, besides MCH services. (Fathalla, 1992).

Without denying the centrality of fertility control to all aspects of reproductive health, women need to be catered to as women and not only as mothers.

An integrated socio-economic approach to population issues is necessary. Women are still viewed as instruments to implement population control policies, rather than subjects with command over their own reproductive rights. That is amply illustrated by the fact that women need their husband's consent to obtain family planning services as also by the fact that adolescents' health needs are completely ignored in the public health system. Furthermore, thousands of poor women are languishing in prison for abortion forced on them by harsh socio-economic conditions (IIDS, 1982) while men go scott free.

Men and adolescents also have need for reproductive health care. They should, as such, not be ignored in formulation of population policies. Family planning and disease control campaigns, sanitation and family planning education, information about venereal and sexually transmitted diseases and their treatment — all need to be directed not only at women but also at men. MCH services, although necessary, are not sufficient to raise women's status. They tend to reinforce women's roles only as mothers and wives. Women need intensive health education about their bodies and their need of "reproductive health". The official media, which survives on the tax payer, should put an end to reinforcing mother/wife stereotypes in advertisements in the name of making money. The first priority for the government media should not be to make money but, rather, to carry key development messages to the masses.

Caring for the siblings - A major responsibility.

Learning early to work.

IX. SUMMARY, CONCLUSIONS AND RECOMMENDATIONS

9.1 Introduction

The objectives of this study as originally set were to update the Statistical Profile of Nepalese Women published in 1979, on the basis of the 1981 and 1991 census; to provide a comparative analysis of the 1971, 1981 and 1991 census data with respect to women; to evaluate the impact of micro-level development interventions on demographic and social variables on the basis of district level census figures; and, finally, to draw policy conclusions. Evaluating micro-level interventions has been extremely difficult because of the dearth of relevant data. Therefore, many policy conclusions could not be drawn on such a basis.

9.2 Demographic Characteristics

1. Nepal's population increased to 18.5 million in 1991 compared to 15 million in 1981, growing by 2.1 percent per annum. The population has grown the quickest in the Tarai due both to internal as well as external in-migration.

2. Nepal's demographic profile is acquiring a younger image as the 0-14 years age category is the quickest growing population group.

3. According to currently published sources the sex ratio, defined as the number of males per 100 females, has altered in favor of women — from 105 in 1981 to 99.5 in 1991. A more detailed analysis of age-specific sex ratios, however, indicates some inconsistencies. The male population has been estimated to be under-enumerated due to its mobility; census population data are being adjusted upwards thereby raising the population growth rate to 2.5 percent and the sex ratio to more than 100.

4. The total marital fertility rate in Nepal, as indicated by the total number of children, ever born to currently married women (TMFR) appears to have stagnated around 6.1 percent since 1971-76. A slight decline is visible among women above the age of 34, after about 4 births. The mean number of children ever born to all women, however, seems to have declined significantly between 1981 and 1991. The major factors in this process are declining early marriages and increasing literacy and education.

131

5. Despite a significant increase in the spread of knowledge about family planning devices, the number of adopters is increasing only very slowly. While 92.7 percent of the population interviewed in 1991 knew about at least one method of family planning, only 24.1 percent were using that knowledge for family planning purposes.

6. Fertility rates are high across all geographical and development regions with the Western and the Central Development Regions being only slightly better off than the three other development regions in terms of total marital fertility rates.

7. Education and urbanization have had a significant, positive effect on fertility reduction.

8. Substantial improvements have been observed in child survival, infant/child/maternal mortality and crude death rates. The sex differential in male/female infant mortality rates shows improvement in the health status of the female infant. But the child mortality rate, that is the number of children dying between zero and five years, is still tilted very heavily against the female child. This indicates substantial discrimination against female children. The maternal mortality rate is improving but it is still one of the highest in the region.

9.3 Social Characteristics

1. The absolute majority of men and women are married by the time they attain 24 years of age. The mean age of marriage, however, has been increasing both for men as well as women. It has gone up from 19.5 years in 1961 to 21.4 years in 1991 for men and from 15.4 to 18 years for women in the same period.

2. Changes are most evident for younger girls. The proportion of married girls in the 10-14 age group has almost been halved from 14.3 percent in 1981 to 7.4 percent in 1991.

3. Such a decline has not, nevertheless, been distributed proportionately among the country's geographic and development regions. The proportion of married girls in the 10-14 age group is still more than 11 percent in the Tarai.

4. The proportion of separated/divorced and widowed female population has increased in 1991 as compared to 1981. It is not clear whether that is a positive or negative change. A more detailed field analysis is needed to cover.that aspect of the phenomenon. The curse of child widowhood and child divorcees is still prevalent.

5. Substantial progress has been made in the field of education in Nepal. Overall, the literacy rate has trebled between 1971 and 1991. The female literacy rate has increased more than six-fold in the same period. However, the differential in the male/female literacy rate is still on the increase.

6. The female literacy appears to be closely related to the overall status of women in various geographical regions of the country as also to the availability of educational facilities. In the Tarai, the male/female differential in literacy rate is uniformly (save the Western Development Region) lower than in other parts of the country.

7. Census recorded enrollment levels are low compared to the 1986 DSS reported figures. Some explanation is called for, in this respect, from the Central Bureau of Statistics. As things stand presently, it is a matter of great concern that only 57.7 percent of boys and 33.6 percent of girls in the 6-15 age group are enrolled in schools.

8. Access to higher levels of education is still greatly limited for girls. Only a small proportion among literate women continue their education beyond the school level.

9.4 Economic Characteristics

1. There is an increasing trend in census-reported female economic activity rates between the censuses, while male economic activity rates demonstrate a declining trend. That may be attributed to definitional problems or the withdrawal of the male population from economic activity for educational purposes. Despite the inaccuracy of census-reported activity rates, such are nevertheless useful in analyzing trends in participation in the organized sector of the national economy.

2. Agriculture is still the major source of employment both for males and females, although the share of the non-agricultural sector in employment is increasing. As in past decades, a relatively larger proportion of women is involved in agriculture as compared to men.

3. The role of non-agricultural sectors as a source of employment is increasing at a faster rate for women than for men. However, the proportion of women in the agriculture labor force has also been on the increase. That could be due to better statistical reporting or to increased migration of men to urban areas for employment purposes. Occupationally, women lag far behind men in the group of administrative and technical and professional workers.

4. Increasing numbers of women are also being pushed out to work in the urban manufacturing sector specially in the textile and wearing apparel sub-sectors where women constitute about 40 percent of the total work force.

5. The employment of women in the manufacturing sector is inversely related to the degree of mechanization and scale of investment. The location of industry also influences employment opportunities for women. Other variables such as degree of industrialisation being the same, women in the Hill areas have a greater probability of obtaining employment in manufacturing than in the Tarai due to the fact that, among many cultural groupings in the Tarai, women are kept isolated from outside contact.

6. The majority of women in the formal manufacturing sector work as semi-skilled and unskilled workers with very few working in the supervisory or management levels. The concentration of women in low paid unskilled jobs may be attributed to low literacy, low skill levels but also to social biases vis-a-vis women's capabilities and aptitudes.

7. According to small surveys of manufacturing sector, most women industrial workers are married and between 14-34 years of age. The overwhelming majority are illiterate and work because of poverty-related reasons.

8. Few women have permanent jobs and receive pay equal to that of their male counterparts. They work in unhealthy physical environment. Many experience health ailments. Only a small minority are trade union members.

9. In the industrial sector women earn less than men because of the system of job classification, mode of employment and exploitation by the factory owners. Women usually earn 20-30 percent less than men as ordinary laborers in agriculture and construction. It was worrisome to note that the differential between male and female wage rates in the agricultural sector was increasing in last few years. Further research is needed in this field to explain this phenomena.

9.5 Political Participation and Access to Positions of Power

1. Political participation may be judged from a two-level perspective: participation in mass political movement in times of crisis and

sustained political activities through time and rise to positions of power. Although in times of crisis women have been mobilized to participate in mass political movements in Nepal, as indeed in other countries in the region, their participation has been sporadic or not sustained through time. Consequently, only a few women have risen to positions of power.

The basic features of the dominant Indo-Aryan culture, the patrilineal inheritance system and extreme concern over the purity of the female body discourage and hinder them for political participation. The political changes of 1990, which ushered in a democratic system of governance, may make a difference to women's political participation and access to positions of power over the long haul. In the short term perspective, however, no change has been visible in that regard.

2. The democratic Constitution (1990) makes it mandatory for political parties to nominate at least 5 percent women candidate for parliamentary elections. In the general elections of 1991, no party put up significantly more than the mandatory minimum of five percent. Many women candidates complained that they were fielded in the more difficult electoral constituencies. Relatively higher proportion of winners among the male condidates corroborates these complaints.

3. The proportion of women in various elected bodies, including parliament, is not very different today than it was during the last years of the partyless panchayat regime. Their membership in the highest legislative body has actually declined from 5.7 percent in the National Panchayat that was elected before the regime ended in April 1990 to 3.4 percent in the House of Representatives, elected in 1991.

4. Complete and recent gender disaggregated figures on employees in government and semi-government institutions are not available. Figures from the 1991 census and the administrative records as of July 1991 indicate an increasing proportion of women serving in administrative jobs. Nevertheless, they are concentrated at the lower rungs of the administrative ladder and have little or no role in the decision making process. Due to HMG's policy of retrenchment of 1992, the proportion of women at the higher reaches of administration may have actually suffered a further decline. Government records have, however, not been updated yet and, as such no definite conclusions can be drawn on that question.

9.6 Emerging Issues

1. One of the most important policy issue that emerges from the foregoing analysis, as far as population policy is concerned, is the stagnating total maternal fertility rate (TMFR). Despite the emphasis on family planning, child and maternal health (MCH) services through seventies and eighties, women still begin thinking about birth control only after they give birth to 4-5 children. Population experts agree, and statistics prove, that child survival, female education, and the age of marriage are the most significant factors affecting fertility behavior. Significant gains have been made in enhancing child survival rates. The mean age of marriage has also been increasing gradually. So, too, are female literacy rates and awareness about family planning devices. Nevertheless, the fertility behavior of women appears to be changing only very slowly.

A major cause for the above is the socio-economic compulsion for women to give birth to at least one son for taking care of her during old age. Women have no access to paternal property, their access to property in their husband's household is conditional on her "sexual" behavior and their "capacity to breed sons". There is no social or economic incentive for a woman to desire to control her "fertility".

All current family planning programs and devices are mostly directed at women. Men, who are more mobile, have greater access to services and economic resources to ensure treatment in case of side effects on health, and who play a decisive role in whether family planning methods should be adopted at all are hardly visible as targets in family planning programs or advertisements.

Besides, women's other health needs related to her reproductive organs are scarly taken care by the medical system. All family planning methods like elsewhere (See Steimen, 1991 for a review) are directed at controlling her fertility rather than enabling her to control her own fertility.

Furthermore, social statistics e.g. education, fertility, marriage age, etc., are seldom disaggregated according to income levels. Consequently, policies and programs are not formulated to deal specifically with different occupational or socio-income groups of households. It has been widely recognized that individuals at the lower end of the income scale view children as "assets" rather than "liabilities". Also, many farmers and laborers, who survive by physical labor, believe that sterilization adversely affects their physical vitality. No programs have been designed to alter such misconceptions.

2. Female education is another emerging issue that cannot be dealt with merely by ad hoc measures such as distribution of free text books or providing a number of scholarships. The real issue is how to change the legal system which disinherits married women from parental property and frees her from the responsibility to look after the parents in their old age and which mandatorily forces the married female out of her parental household. The core questions also concern correcting society's perception of girls as "liabilities" and glorification of women only as "mothers". Similarly, they are also related to changing a religious belief system that compel females to be married at an early age and couples to breed sons for their after-life salvation.

3. Urbanization is resulting in serval parallel trends. A substantial proportion of women are marginalized from active economic life and are being transformed into housewives in the narrowest sense of the term. As long as family farms predominate as the household's primary source of income/livelihood, women participate equally with their menfolks in farming activities. Although that is not recognized in official statistics, they do have an economic role to play and society has thus to recognize it, one way or another. With the shifting of the production process and the work arena to the factory or the marketplace, an increasing number of women find themselves constricted within a purely domestic perimeter. A comparative analysis of rural and urban female economic activity rates indicates that a relatively larger percentage of urban women are withdrawing from active economic life conforming to the similar trends observed in other countries at the early stages of urbanisation and industrialisation.

On the other hand, an increasing number of women are being forced to work as factory workers in the manufacturing sector and this increasing female labor force is being subjected to appalling working environment and intense exploitation at the factory floor. As they come out to work, in the process they are enhancing their income and earning some amount of independence from their families. Yet, most of such workers are relatively young, overwhelmingly uneducated and enter the work force compelled by poverty. They are vulnerable to exploitation on the factory floor by their supervisors and owners due to the patriarchal value system that prevails in Nepalese society. Households that send women to work outside the family enterprise to factory floor specially as laborers, lose their social status in the public eye. As individuals, working women may make some marginal gains in terms of increase in income and in decision making roles within the household; but they lose out in the public arena as their household is held to be downgraded in social status. These are complex social processes at work here and it is therefore difficult to accurately assess their overall impact.

4. Mass communications media, even in the official sector, are not being used adequately to counter outdated religious or social value systems that are biased against women. Development messages propagating social changes (e.g. "treat girls equally with boys") are countered by commercial advertisements projecting women as sex symbols and by movies and tele-serials that glorify sacrifices by women for their sons and husbands. The government does not appear to have a standard on social behavior or a code of commercial advertisements even for the government media.

5. Gender-specific statistics are still limited and scattered. For example, we still do not know how much difference there is between male and female infant mortality rates in urban and rural areas. That is vital to judge whether urbanization reduces discrimination against female infants. In many surveys (e.g. the NFH Survey, 1991) samples are too small for gender disaggregated analysis. It is extremely difficult, for example, to obtain general disaggregated statistics on government employees. No information is available on development programs at the district level, even for those in the government sector.

9.7 Recommendations

1. As far as fertility control is concerned it is time to think about taking appropriate measures to separate women's economic security from her "sex" and her "capacity to bear sons". All daughters, whether married or otherwise, should be accorded rights to parental property equal to that of her brothers. Such a legal provision may not, by itself, trigger overnight change in the social status of women. It should, however, definitely provide women the strength to fight her social battles. Currently, economic compulsions as well as the social climate apply pressure on her to produce sons. Only equal right to parental

property will ensure for her the necessary economic and psychological security to ensure reduced fertility.

2. Any initiative on legal transfer of public assets to the people, e.g. public lands and forests, must include women, too. Being equal owners of such assets will facilitate their direct access to valuable resources and thus reduce their economic compulsion to give birth to sons.

3. Family planning programs should also be targeted at men — not only to women. It is, after all, men who have the decisive voice in household matters. It is they who have access to resources. Finally, it is once again men whose life even during their old age is ensured, even without sons.

4. Special programs should be tailored to the specific needs and cultural sensitivities of the numerous socio-economic groupings that constitute Nepal's population.

5. As far as female education is concerned, informal education programs, such as "Cheli-Beti", designed specially for working girls should be disseminated as widely as possible, covering both the urban as well as rural areas. Poverty obliges many parents, even in urban and sub-urban areas, to have their daughters work. Yet, there are no schools or other educational facilities even in urban centers where working girls can pursue academic studies. It is, of course, natural that they cannot attend night schools for obvious security reasons. The operation of schools that open for two-three hours, beginning at various time period of the day, might mitigate that problem somewhat.

6. Concerted media programs are required to attack outdated social and religious value systems that are biased against females. Programs must be targeted at such customs/beliefs as early marriage for girls and the idea that parents will receive salvation after death only through "sons". Even that, however, would not be adequate. The official media needs to develop a code of behavior on the type of female image to be projected and all advertisements or stories which do not conform to such an desired public media projection should be rejected outright. Images glorifying women in their roles as sisters and mothers should not be allowed to be replaced by those that treat women as sex symbols. It is understood that in the present day media explosion, effective controls cannot be imposed on the external media. That, however, should not be an excuse for the official media to emulate their example. Rather, they should attempt to counter such harmful messages or

distortion in projection of the female with appropriate messages and / or programs.

7. Greater attention needs to be paid to ensure that women are safe in the factory or work place, to facilitate their access to modern education and training schemes without bias or discrimination, and to formulate policies promoting employment for women in such a manner that they are not marginalized by the marketization of subsistence agriculture and village crafts.

8. All available statistics, e.g. census results, should be broken down by gender at the processing stage and the results published along with other statistics. Reprocessing large data sets is very expensive and, as such, women's advocacy groups cannot afford to finance such a felt need. Similarly, all data generated by government machinery should be made available along with accompanying gender breakdowns.

Annex

Annex A. Time Use Pattern of Female Household Members by Income Group (15 years and above)

(Time in hours per day)

Activities / Income Strata / Region	Urban Areas				Rural Areas			
	Poor		Not Poor		Poor		Not Poor	
	Hill	Tarai	Hill	Tarai	Hill	Tarai	Hill	Tarai
Conventional Economic	2.67	1.36	1.79	1.30	2.64	1.71	2.62	1.50
Agriculture	1.57	0.61	0.60	0.45	2.21	1.31	2.20	1.30
Production	0.15	0.06	0.18	0.06	0.06	0.03	0.05	0.02
Construction	-	0.02	0.02	0.03	0.05	0.01	0.03	0.01
Trade & Commerce	0.12	0.06	0.34	0.29	0.05	0.13	0.14	0.08
Service	0.83	0.61	0.65	0.47	0.27	0.23	0.20	0.09
Subsistence Economic	1.97	1.38	1.18	1.01	2.58	1.91	2.42	1.68
Fuel & Fodder collection and fetching water	1.73	1.09	1.00	0.79	2.07	1.28	1.92	1.23
House repair and construction	0.02	0.03	0.01	0.02	2.02	0.05	0.04	0.04
Hunting and gathering	0.09	0.13	0.08	0.09	0.22	0.27	0.20	0.16
Food processing	0.13	0.13	0.08	0.11	0.27	0.31	0.26	0.25
TOTAL ECONOMIC (1 + 2)	4.64	2.44	2.97	2.31	5.22	3.62	5.04	3.18
Domestic Work	5.26	6.71	5.65	6.65	5.24	5.94	5.95	5.90
Childcare	0.94	1.53	0.74	1.31	1.01	1.08	1.50	0.96
Other	4.32	5.18	4.91	5.34	4.23	4.86	4.45	4.94
WORK BURDEN (1 + 2 + 3)	9.90	9.15	8.62	8.96	10.46	9.56	10.99	9.08

Source: NRB, Multipurpose Household Budget Survey, 1984/85.
Special Tabulations

Annex B : Nominal Wage Rates In Four Urban Towns of Nepal
(FY 1980/81 - 1992/93)

Catagory	Agriculture (per day)		Industrial Labor (per month)			Laborersa/ (per day)			Manson (per day)	
Fiscal Year	Male	Female	High-Skilled	Skilled	Semi-Skilled	Un-Skilled	Male	Female	Skilled	Semi-Skilled
Kathmandu										
1980/81	15	10	-	290	0	200	-	-	26	25
1981/82	15	10	-	334	0	230	-	-	31	29
1982/83	20	15	-	377	0	260	-	-	35	33
1983/84	20	15	-	377	0	260	-	-	40	38
1984/85	22	18	-	452	0	325	-	-	45	40
1985/86	25	20	-	452	0	325	-	-	50	45
1986/87	25	20	598	452	365	325	30	-	60	55
1987/88	35	35	698	552	465	425	35	35	68	63
1988/89	40	40	873	690	582	532	40	37	78	73
1989/90	43	40	876	690	582	532	42	40	82	78
1990/91	55	43	1141	958	850	800	55	47	108	98
1991/92	60	45	1141	958	850	800	60	53	118	105
1992/93	70	45	1321	1134	1025	975	70	63	160	145
Bhairahawa										
1980/81	8	8	-	390	-	200	-	-	20	19
1981/82	9	9	-	322	-	222	-	-	22	19
1982/83	10	9	-	378	-	260	-	-	29	24
1983/84	13	11	-	378	-	260	-	-	31	28
1984/85	13	11	-	427	-	303	-	-	35	32
1985/86	15	12	-	452	-	325	-	-	44	39
1986/87	19	16	698	552	465	425	-	-	49	40
1987/88	24	21	711	577	490	450	24	21	55	43
1988/89	27	23	811	646	549	504	20	17	60	55
1989/90	30	28	873	690	582	532	20	17	65	58
1990/91	33	33	1141	958	850	800	33	30	75	65
1991/92	38	38	1141	958	850	800	38	38	80	70
1992/93	40	40	1321	1134	1025	975	40	40	80	70

Contd...

Annex B : Nominal Wage Rates In Four Urban Towns of Nepal
(FY 1980/81 - 1992/93)

Catagory	Agriculture (per day)		Industrial Labor (per month)			Laborersa/ (per day)			Manson (per day)	
Fiscal Year	Male	Female	High-Skilled	Skilled	Semi-Skilled	Un-Skilled	Male	Female	Skilled	Semi-Skilled
Biratnagar										
1980/81	10	9	-	350	-	260	-	-	22	20
1981/82	12	11	-	350	-	260	-	-	23	21
1982/83	12	11	-	416	-	260	-	-	29	25
1983/84	15	14	-	452	-	260	-	-	31	25
1984/85	18	16	-	452	-	310	-	-	36	31
1985/86	19	19	-	485	-	325	-	-	43	38
1986/87	20	20	631	552	398	358	20	20	48	43
1987/88	23	21	698	552	465	425	22	21	55	50
1988/89	25	22	873	690	58	532	25	22	63	58
1989/90	28	27	873	690	582	532	28	25	70	65
1990/91	33	29	1141	958	850	800	35	32	78	73
1991/92	38	33	1141	958	850	800	43	38	85	78
1992/93	43	38	1425	1215	1059	980	48	43	95	8
Nepalgunj										
1980/81	9	8	-	322	-	242	-	-	22	19
1981/82	12	10	-	355	-	268	-	-	24	22
1982/83	13	12	-	377	-	312	-	-	27	24
1983/84	15	12	-	414	-	315	-	-	28	25
1984/85	16	13	-	442	-	319	-	-	30	28
1985/86	17	15	-	452	-	325	-	-	35	30
1986/87	17	16	598	452	365	325	-	-	47	39
1987/88	21	21	644	496	423	403	-	-	55	45
1988/89	28	23	782	615	531	506	-	-	63	55
1989/90	33	30	873	690	582	532	33	-	70	63
1990/91	38	33	1141	958	850	800	38	35	83	70
1991/92	39	33	1141	958	850	800	39	35	108	88
1992/93	39	33	1246	1059	950	900	43	38	125	100

Source: Nepal Rastra Bank
a/ Mostly construction workers and loaders
"-" indicates not available

144

REFERENCES AND SOURCES OF STATISTICS

ACHARYA MEENA
1979 Statistical Profile of Nepalese Women: A Critical Review *The Status of Women in Nepal*, Vol. I, Part 1, Center for Economic Development and Administration, Kathmandu

....

1981 The Maithili Women of Sirsia, *The Status of Women in Nepal* Vol II Part 1. Center for Economic Development and Administration, Kathmandu.

....

1989 Poverty and Women in Nepal. (Mimeo Submitted to the World Bank).

....

"1993 Political Restructuring & Women's Development" Lecture in University of California, Berkley. (Mimeo).

....

1994 "Political Participation of Women in Nepal" in Chowdhari N. and Nelson B (edt.) *Women and Politics World-Wide* Yale University Press.

ACHARYA MEENA & LYNN BENNETT
1981 The Rural Women of Nepal: An Aggregate Analysis and Summary of 8 Village Studies, *The Status of Women in Nepal*, Vol. II, Part 9, Center for Economic Development and Administration, Tribhuvan University, Kathmandu.

....

1983 *Women and the Subsistence Sector: Economic Participation and Household Decision making in Nepal:* World Bank Staff Working Papers, No. 562, Washington, D.C., U.S.A.

ASIAN DEVELOPMENT BANK/HMG
1985 Nepal Industrial Sector Study, Manila.

ASMITA PUBLICATIONS
1992 *Asmita*, December, Kathmandu.

BANERJEE, NIRMALA (edt.)
1991 *Indian Women in a Changing Industrial Scenario,* Sage Publications, New Delhi.

BANGLADESH BUREAU OF STATISTICS
1993 Women and Men in Bangladesh, Facts and Figures, 1992, Dhaka.

1992 Statistical Year Book of Bangladesh, Dhaka.

BOSERUP, ESTER
1970(a) *Women's Role in Economic Development* St.Martins Press, New York.

1970(b) Preface in *Women and National Development : The Complexities of Change.* The Wellesley Editorial Committee, Chicago Press, Chicago.

BASNET, PRABHA
1992 "Status of Women Workers in Some Industries" (Nepali) A Paper Presented to the *Tripartite National Workshop* on the Role of Labor Administration in Promotion of Employment and Welfare of Women Workers in Nepal, January, 1992. Ministry of Labor and Social Welfare, Women Development Division and ILO, Kathmandu.

BENNETT LYNN
1979 The Parbatiya Women of Bakundol *The Status of Women in Nepal* Vol. I, Part 2, Center for Economic Development and Administration, Tribhuvan University, Kathmandu.

....

1983 *"Dangerous Wives and Sacred Sisters"*, Columbia University Press, New York.

BENERIA, LOURDES
1982 "The Sexual Division of Labor in Rural Societies" Praeger, New York.

CENTRAL BUREAU OF STATISTICS
1961, 1971, 1981 and 1991 Definitions and Regulations on the Nepal National Census (Nepali), Kathmandu.

....
1976, The Demographic Sample Survey of Nepal, 1974-75, Survey Method and Findings, Kathmandu.

....
1977, The Demographic Sample Survey of Nepal, Second Year Survey, 1976, Kathmandu.

....
1977 The Analysis of the Population Statistics of Nepal, Kathmandu.

....
1978, The Demographic Sample Survey of Nepal, Third Year Survey 1977-78, Kathmandu.

....
1985, Inter-censal Changes of Some Key Census Variables, Nepal 1952/54-1981, Kathmandu.

......r...
1987 Population Monograph of Nepal, Kathmandu.

....
1993, The Analysis of the 1991 Population Census (based on advance tables), Kathmandu.

....
1976/77, 1986/87, 1990/91 Survey of Manufacturing Industries, CBS, Kathmandu.

CHOWDHARI, NAJMA
1994 "Women as Political Actors in Bangladesh: Gender Issues and Politics in a Patriarchy" in Chowdhari N. and Barbara Nelson (edt.) *Women and Politics World-wide,* Yale University Press, New Haven, USA.

COTTAGE AND VILLAGE INDUSTRIES DEVELOPMENT BOARD
1990 Progress Report, Kathmandu.

DIXIT, SHANTA
1992 "Sexual Diseases Transmitted by Men" in *Asmita,* December, 1992, Kathmandu.

ELECTION COMMISSION
1987 National and District Level Election Reports, 1986/87, Kathmandu.

....
1992 National and District Level Election Reports, 1991/92, Kathmandu.

ECONOMIC SERVICES CENTRE LTD.
1990 Socio-Economic Impact of CSI-Phase I - A Survey Study Report - Prepared for NRB, Kathmandu.

FEIJOO, MARIA DEL CARMEN
1994 "From Family Ties to Political Action: Women's Experiences in Argentina"in Chowdhari N. and Barbara Nelson (edt.) *Women and Politics World-wide*, Yale University Press, New Haven, USA.

FAMILY PLANNING, MATERNAL AND CHILD HEALTH/MOH
1991 Nepal Fertility, Family Planning and Health Survey, Submitted by NIV Joint Venture, Kathmandu.

FATHALLA, M.F.
1992 Reproductive Health in the World: Two Decades of Progress and the Challenge Ahead, in WHO. *Reproductive Health. A Key to a Brighter Future.* Biennial Report 1990-91. Special 20th Anniversary Issue.

GHARTI CHHETRY, R.K.
1994 "Levels and Trends in Fertility in Nepal" in *Tathyanka Gatibidhi* - 1993/94 Nov.-March, (2050/51 Marg - Phalgun) CBS, Kathmandu.

GIELE, JANET ZOLLINGER
1977 Introduction : The Status of Women in Comparative Perspective in *Women's Roles and Status in Eight Countries.* by Giele and Smock,(edt.) John Wiley and Sons, New York.

INSTITUTE FOR INTEGRATED DEVELOPMENT STUDIES
1982 *Women in Prison*, Kathmandu.

ISLAM, R./SHRESTHA, R.P.
1986 *Employment Expansion Through Cottage Industries in Nepal: Potentials and Constraints;* ILO-ARTEP, New Delhi, India.

JOSHI, A.
1985 "Women's Participation in Carpet Industry: with special Reference To Kathmandu District" *Dissertation*: Tribhuvan University, Nepal.

KASARDA, JOHN D., JOHN O.G. BILLY AND KIRSTEN WEST
1986 *Status Enhancement and Fertility* Academic Press INC. New York.

KEMP, SHARAN F.
1986 "How Women's Work is Perceived: Hunger or Humiliation" in James W. Bjorkman (edt.) *The Changing Division of Labor in South Asia;* The Riverdale Company, Publishers Riverdale, M.A., U.S.A.

LAKHEY, BIMALA AND D.S. MALLA
1992 "Septic Abortion and Maternal Mortality" (Mimeo), Kathmandu.

LIM, LINDA Y.C.
1983 "Multinational Export Factories and Women Workers in the Third World: A Review of Theory and Evidence." In Nagat M. El-Sanabary (edt.). *Women and Work in the Third World: The Impact of Industrialization and Global Economic Interdependence,* Conference Proceedings, 6-7 May 1982 and 14-15 April 1983, University of California, Berkeley.

MANIKYAMBA, P.
1986 "The Participatory Predicament : Women in Indian Politics" in James W. Bjorkman (edt.) *The Changing Division of Labor in South Asia.* Riverdale Company Publishers. Riverdale, Maryland, USA.

MINISTRY OF HEALTH
1991 Maternal and Child Health: Management Issues at Community Health Post and District Levels, MOH/HMG.

NATIONAL PLANNING COMMISSION, HMG, KATHMANDU
Fifth Five Year Plan, 1975/76-1979/80.
Sixth Five Year Plan, 19800/81-1985/86.
Seventh Five Year Plan, 1985/86-1989/90.
Eighth Five Year Plan, 1991/92-1996/97.

NEW ERA
1986, Nepal Fertility & Mortality Survey - A Preliminary Report 1987, Kathmandu.

NEPAL FAMILY PLANNING, MATERNAL AND CHILD HEALTH/MOH
1977 Nepal Fertility Survey 1976, First Report, Kathmandu.

NEPAL RASTRA BANK
1988 *Multipurpose Household Budget Survey: A Study on Income Distribution, Employment, and Consumption Patterns in Nepal;* Kathmandu.

NIRAULA, BADRI
1994 (A) *Notes on Use of Labor Force Data in the Changed Perspective,* Kathmandu (Mimeo).

....
1994 (B) "Internal Migration" in *Tathyanka Gatibidhi* - 1993/94 Nov.-March, (2050/51 Marg-Phalgun) CBS, Kathmandu.

NIJAMATI KITAB KHANA
1991 The Law of the Land (Muluki Ain) with all Amendments, Kathmandu.

OJHA, H.K.
1984, "Women's Participation In Handloom Industry At Kirtipur Village" *Dissertation*: Tribhuvan University, Nepal.

RANA, M.S.J.B./SHAH A.J.
1987 *Role of Women in Nepal's Industrial Development: Status, Constraints, Opportunities and Prospects;* Vol. I & II. HMG/Nepal - UNIDO/Vienna Project.

RESEARCH CENTRE FOR EDUCATIONAL INNOVATION AND DEVELOPMENT (CERID)
1986(a) *Women's Participation in Non-formal Education Programme in Nepal;* T.U., Kathmandu.

....
1986(b) Education of Girls and Women in Nepal, T.U., Kathmandu.

ROSENFIELD A., M.F. FATHALLA, A. GERMAIN AND C.L. INDSISO(edt.)
1989. *Women's Health in the third World. The impact of unwanted Pregnancy,* Supplement to *International Journal of Gynecology and Obstitries.* IWHC Publications. No. 3 1989.

SALAFF, JANET W.
1981 *Working Daughters of Hong Kong*, Cambridge University Press, Cambridge.

SHRESTHA, MOTISHOVA
1990 Participation of Women in Industrial Development-A Paper (Nepali) presented in the *Seminar on Women and Development*, organised by the Ministry of Labor and Social Welfare, May-1990.

SHRESTHA, NEERU
1983 *Women's Employment in Industrial Sector, Nepal;* CEDA, Tribhuvan University, Kathmandu.

SIEGEL, LENNY
1983 "Employment of Women in Export Assembly of High Technology Electronics in Asia." In El-Sanabary (edt.), *op.cit.*

STEIMEN, GLORIA
1993 *"The War Against Women"* Ballantine Books, New York, U.S.A.

THACKER, PRAVHA
1992 *Technology Womens Work and Status:* The Case of the Carpet Industry in Nepal. Mountain Regeneration and Employment - Discussion Paper Series, 21. International Centre for Integrated Mountain Development, Kathmandu.

TULADHAR, JAYANTI, GUBHAJU, B.B., STOECKEL, JOHN
1977, "The Population of Nepal: Structure and Change", University of California Press, Berkeley.

UNITED NATIONS
1987 "Review of Occupation and Industry Classification Experience in Three Countries and Comments on the 1987 Proposed Revision of the International Standard Classification of Occupation from the Perspective of Women's Concerns" *Fourteenth International Conference of Labor Statisticians,* Geneva, 28 Oct. - 6 Nov. 1987.

....

1991 The World's Women - Trends and Statistics 1970 - 1990, New York.

....

1991 Population and Housing Censuses of Various Countries. New York.

....
1991 Demographic Year Book, New York.

....
1993 The Human Development Report, New York.

UNFPA
1991 Inventory of Population Projects in Developing Countries Around the World, 1990/91, New York.

UNICEF
1992 Children and Women of Nepal: A Situation Analysis, Kathmandu.

UNIDO
1988 *The Current and Prospective Contribution of Women to Nepal's Industrial Developement:* Regional and Country Studies Branch, Industrial Policy and Perspective Division.

WORLD BANK
1991 World Development Report, Oxford University Press, USA.

....
1992 World Development Report, Oxford University Press, USA.

....
1993 World Development Report, Oxford University Press, USA.

WORLD HEALTH ORGANIZATION/HMG
1992 Research Report on Prevention of Maternal Mortality in Hospitals of Nepal, Kathmandu.